THE DIAMOND SMUGGLERS

Ian Lancaster Fleming was born in London on 28 May 1908 and was educated at Eton College before spending a formative period studying languages in Europe. His first job was with Reuters news agency, followed by a brief spell as a stockbroker. On the outbreak of the Second World War he was appointed assistant to the Director of Naval Intelligence, Admiral Godfrey, where he played a key part in British and Allied espionage operations.

After the war he joined Kemsley Newspapers as Foreign Manager of the *Sunday Times,* running a network of correspondents who were intimately involved in the Cold War. His first novel, *Casino Royale,* was published in 1953 and introduced James Bond, Special Agent 007, to the world. The first print run sold out within a month. Following this initial success, he published a Bond title every year until his death. Raymond Chandler hailed him as 'the most forceful and driving writer of thrillers in England.' The fifth title, *From Russia with Love,* was particularly well received and sales soared when President Kennedy named it as one of his favourite books. The Bond novels have sold more than sixty million copies and inspired a hugely successful film franchise which began in 1962 with the release of *Dr No* starring Sean Connery as 007.

The Bond books were written in Jamaica, a country Fleming fell in love with during the war and where he built a house, 'Goldeneye'. He married Anne Rothermere in 1952. His story about a magical car, written in 1961 for their only child Caspar, went on to become the well-loved novel and film, *Chitty Chitty Bang Bang.* Fleming died of heart failure on 12 August 1964.

www.ianfleming.com

BOOKS BY IAN FLEMING

The James Bond Books

Casino Royale

Live and Let Die

Moonraker

Diamonds are Forever

From Russia with Love

Dr No

Goldfinger

For Your Eyes Only

Thunderball

The Spy Who Loved Me

On Her Majesty's Secret Service

You Only Live Twice

The Man with the Golden Gun

Octopussy and The Living Daylights

Non-fiction

The Diamond Smugglers

Thrilling Cities

Children's

Chitty Chitty Bang Bang

IAN FLEMING

THE DIAMOND SMUGGLERS

WITH AN INTRODUCTION BY

Fergus Fleming

VINTAGE BOOKS
London

IAN FLEMING PUBLICATIONS LIMITED

Published by Vintage 2013

4 6 8 10 9 7 5

Copyright © Gildrose Productions Ltd. 1957
Introduction Copyright © Fergus Fleming 2009

First published by Jonathan Cape in 1957

Vintage
20 Vauxhall Bridge Road,
London SW1V 2SA

penguin.co.uk/vintage

Vintage is part of the Penguin Random House group of companies whose addresses
can be found at global.penguinrandomhouse.com

The Random House Group Limited Reg. No. 954009

A CIP catalogue record for this book
is available from the British Library

ISBN 9780099578192

Printed and bound in Great Britain by Clays Ltd, St Ives plc

CONTENTS

INTRODUCTION

WHEN THE DIAMOND SMUGGLERS WAS FIRST PUBLISHED Ian Fleming had a copy bound for his own library. On the flyleaf, as was his custom, he wrote a short paragraph describing its genesis. It started with the alarming words: 'This was written in 2 weeks in Tangiers, April 1957.' As the ensuing tale of woe made clear, he didn't consider it his finest fortnight. He ended with the dismissive verdict: 'It is adequate journalism but a poor book and necessarily rather "contrived" though the facts are true.'

It should have been a golden opportunity. The Sunday Times had acquired a manuscript from an ex-MI5 agent called John Collard who had been employed by De Beers to break a diamond smuggling ring. Fleming, whose Diamonds Are Forever had been one of the hits of 1956, was invited to bring it to life. Treasure, travel, cunning and criminality:

here were the things he loved. Flying to Tangier – home to every shade of murky dealing – he spent ten days interviewing Collard, for whom he had already prepared the romantic pseudonym 'John Blaize' and the equally romanticised job description of 'diamond spy'.

The glister tarnished swiftly. He visited neither the diamond fields of Namibia or Sierra Leone, with which the story was primarily concerned, but sat in the Hotel Minzah typing up his notes. It rained constantly and he found the landscape dull. There was little scope for literary flair, his more extravagant flourishes being blue-pencilled routinely by Collard. When the final version was serialised by the Sunday Times in September and October 1957 further material had to be excised under threat of legal action by De Beers. 'It was a good story until all the possible libel was cut out,' Fleming wrote gloomily.

Yet if The Diamond Smugglers was a disappointment to its author it still contains flashes of Fleming-esque magic. Amidst the Tangerian alleys he strays unerringly to the thieves' kitchen of Socco Chico, '[where] crooks and smugglers and dope pedlars congregate, and a pretty villainous gang they are.' Travelling with 'Blaize' to the Atlantic coast he encounters a forest of radio masts – still one of the world's communication hubs – where they 'could imagine the air above us filled with whispering voices.' Later, as they walk down the beach they stumble (literally) on a shoal of Portuguese Men of War driven ashore by a storm. Alone on the tip of Africa, with the coast stretching 200 miles to Casablanca, the sea running uninterrupted to America, and a carpet of jellyfish beneath their feet, the two men conduct what has to be one of the most surreal interviews in history. 'It amused Blaize to stamp on their poisonous-looking violet bladders as we went along,' Fleming wrote, 'and his talk was punctuated with what sounded like small-calibre revolver shots.'

Today The Diamond Smugglers is one of Fleming's least known works. But in its time it was one of his most commercially valuable. It sold in its hundreds of thousands. No sooner was it in print than Rank bought a film treatment for the princely sum of £12,500. (Further misery: he had to split the proceeds with Collard and the Sunday Times.) Nothing came of the project. But in 1965, by which time Fleming was dead and Bond a worldwide phenomenon, it flared briefly into life. Items concerning its progress featured in the press: a thrusting young producer had it in hand; 'John Blaize' would emerge as a new Bond-like character; Kingsley Amis had been hired to write the script; the drama would be intense. After a while the announcements became slightly plaintive. And then they stopped.

More than forty years later it remains something of a conundrum; a journalistic chore that its author disliked but which nevertheless became a best-seller and very nearly his first film; a book that is neither travelogue nor thriller but combines the discarded hopes of both; a tale of international intrigue and exploding jellyfish that leads to the final question: 'Who wouldn't rather play golf?' It is a wry, unplaceable thing, but all the more interesting for that. Certainly it doesn't live up to Fleming's self-damning critique. Take this sentence from the opening paragraph:

'One day in April 1957 I had just answered a letter from an expert in unarmed combat writing from a cover address in Mexico City, and I was thanking a fan in Chile, when my telephone rang.' If you're given a line like that you can only read on.

Fergus Fleming, 2009

PREFACE

THE FISHING AND GAME-WATCHING HOLIDAY IN THE St. Lucia estuary of Zululand was something I had been looking forward to for a very long time. I had just locked the front door of my house in Johannesburg and was getting into the car for the 450-mile drive to the coast when a grey uniformed postman pedalled up with a telegram. I felt a strong temptation to leave the thing unopened, but luckily thought better of it and found it was from Ian Fleming. Fleming's cryptic message was to lead to one of the pleasantest episodes I have had in a varied career and, what was more important, it involved no interference with my trip to Zululand. Fleming merely wished to know what time and where he could contact me by telephone within the next few days. I cabled back 'St. Lucia Hotel Zululand any evening' and, hardly expecting to hear any more, off I drove with my fishing-rods.

I did, in fact, hear quite a lot more, and after a spate of telegrams between London, St. Lucia and Tangier my meeting with Fleming took place just as he describes. On arrival at the El Minzah Hotel, Tangier, I was greeted by the porter with a note which I still have (alas, I have been taught to keep even the most trivial notes!):

'Welcome! I'm in Room 52. Would you give me a ring when you arrive and we'll have a drink. Good to have you here.'

IAN F.

This seemed a promising beginning and I was not to be disappointed. Fleming's company during the next ten days or so was a stimulating experience.

One of the things I liked about him was his informality. He was known to quite a few members of the British community in Tangier and he automatically included me in the various luncheon and dinner parties they gave for him.

This is where my 'cover' came in, and now is my opportunity to offer an apology for my part in the deception practised on a lot of charming people who were much too well-bred to ask awkward questions at the time.

Polite formalities at the Minzah soon gave way to down-to-earth discussion about the form and scope of this book.

I made it plain from the start that, although the decision to tell the story was taken entirely on my own authority, I wanted to be sure that the published version would be free from security and all other objections. Ian Fleming, as a former naval intelligence officer, entirely agreed and, as

things turned out, had to tone down a few of my rather
critical opinions, and some interesting names and details had
to be withheld altogether. It was my desire that the story
would offend no one but the crooks; and that, I think, has
been achieved. To some extent Fleming was helped by the
fact that I had brought with me a private diary of my own
activities which I had been compiling in idle moments over a
long period, and it was these notes and my memories which
he has most skilfully forged into a connected narrative.

This bizarre meeting in Tangier had its origins in
November 1953, when Sir Percy Sillitoe had retired as head
of MI5. He told me when he asked me to join *him* how
it had all come about. He was enjoying his leisure at East-
bourne when a letter arrived from Sir Reginald Leeper, the
former British Ambassador, and then, as now, Chairman of
the London Committee of De Beers Consolidated Mines.

Sir Ernest Oppenheimer had asked him, as he put it, to
see if Sir Percy would be interested in giving his advice and
assistance on a matter which he hoped to have an opportunity
of putting before Sir Percy.

'The matter' turned out to be the enormous illicit traffic
in diamonds, and Sir Ernest Oppenheimer's desire that Sir
Percy should set up an organization to combat it.

Who would not have been interested? Sir Percy at once
flew out to Muizenburg, just outside Capetown, where Sir
Ernest was spending his summer holiday.

Sir Percy was immensely struck by Sir Ernest Oppenheimer – by his charm and by his razor-sharp mind – and
he couldn't understand why his biography had never been

written: the story of the man who started in Kimberley in 1902 as the representative of a small diamond firm and who, in less than fifty years, built up the largest combined diamond, gold, coal and copper empire in the world.

It seems that Sir Ernest was indulgent about Sir Percy's total ignorance of the diamond industry up to the moment when diamonds get set into engagement rings. He explained the basic process of *mining* and marketing diamonds and the points at which, in his opinion, there were possibilities of leakage. He then suggested that Sir Percy should make a personal examination of the mines themselves all over the African Continent and return to Johannesburg and report on the prospects of plugging the leaks at least at the producing end of the business.

Sir Percy agreed and, in March 1954, set off with two of the team he had by that time selected, on an itinerary which in six weeks included Accra, Aquatia, Freetown, Yengema, Leopoldville, Tshaikapa, Bakwanga, Luluabourg, Dundo, Elizabethville, Lushoto, Dar-es-Salaam, Mwadui, Lusaka, Salisbury, Pretoria and Johannesburg – a journey I am astonished that, at the age of sixty-six, he managed to complete without collapsing by the wayside.

Unfortunately there had already been leakage to the Press, as the amusing cartoon reproduced shows; and Sir Percy thought it advisable to call on his old friend Mr. Swart, Minister of Justice, and also Major-General J. A. Brink, the Commissioner of the South African Police, and tell them in confidence of his assignment. He gave them his assurance that in no circumstances would he employ an

agent or informer for use in South Africa without the consent
of the Commissioner of Police. He also endeavoured to
meet Brigadier Rademeyer, then head of the CED. It was
he who had set up the Diamond Detectives branch of
the South African Police with headquarters at Kimberley.
As ill luck would have it he was on holiday at that time,
and it came as an unwelcome blow to Sir Percy to read in one
of the South African newspapers that Brigadier Rademeyer
was very critical of his proposed and alleged activities
and had commented adversely on the fact that he had not
paid him a visit. But I must say that later, when IDSO
(we called ourselves the International Diamond Security
Organization) was in full operation, all of us found Brigadier
Rademeyer most co-operative and helpful, particularly when
he had succeeded Major-General Brink as Commissioner
of Police.

In his six weeks' tour of the diamond mines Sir Percy
told me that he was dazzled by the thousands upon thousands
of diamonds, from pea to walnut in size, which were laid
out for his inspection at the different mines, and he began
to absorb some of the sinister fascination which has always
surrounded these coldest of all gems. Objects so small and
at the same time so valuable were obviously destined for
ever to have crime, and even murder, attached to them and,
having seen the way they were handled up to the moment
when they were posted to London for sale by the Diamond
Corporation, Sir Percy said he was only surprised that the
annual leakage by theft, smuggling and illicit digging did
not add up to many more millions than the figures which

had been given him. Not only Sir Percy but all of us acquired real admiration for the various company officials through whose hands pass every day gems worth perhaps a hundred times their annual salary.

Sir Percy's plans were approved and he flew back to London and took me on to complete his team, and that was how, three years later, I came to meet Ian Fleming in Tangier. I treated my time in Tangier rather like the reward of a chocolate after swallowing a dose of medicine. The main difference was that Tangier was unexpected. Working for the International Diamond Security Organization was not 'fun'. The only 'prize' was the satisfaction of Sir Percy Sillitoe – a man who is not easily satisfied, but who, from time to time, sent us signals of encouragement as we set about our main tasks. These were, first, to increase security at the mines and, secondly, to discover beyond doubt the major channels of leakage to Europe, the Middle East and the Iron Curtain countries.

The latter task was the more difficult of the two, but at least we had the advantage of being able to adopt one method of attack – buying from the smugglers themselves – which was not available to the police forces owing to lack of money. Our undercover buying in Liberia and Rhodesia was not expected to lead directly to convictions, but it did result in the penetration and exposure of whole networks of smuggling rings which had hitherto been hidden.

The normal police system of attacking the IDB [Illicit Diamond Buying] problem had in the past largely relied on the 'trap' method whereby a selected suspect is approached by a plain clothes policeman and invited to buy 'police' diamonds. At the critical moment, when the suspect falls for the policeman's offer, he is arrested. The operation is concluded without gleaning a single item of genuine intelligence.

The persistent operation of the trap method no doubt served the useful purpose of preventing IDB from establishing the upper hand in countries like South Africa, but the police inevitably came in for severe criticism from the Bench after instituting proceedings based on a trap. Thus, in the High Court of South-West Africa in September 1953, Mr. Justice Claasens, in finding a father and son named Vlok not guilty of IDB, said there were two kinds of trap. One was for those suspected of dealing in diamonds and the other was to induce innocent people to do what they normally would not do. This case, he pronounced, was of the latter type, with the additional aggravation that the decoy was a relation of the accused. 'These cases,' said the Judge, 'come close to the prostitution of the police and of the Courts.' We in IDSO agreed with this view and thought very little of trapping of any sort.

During its short life, IDSO's relations with most police forces, particularly those of British Colonial territories and protectorates in Africa, were extremely happy. Most of these forces had more serious problems on their hands than IDB, but of those plagued by the latter, Sierra Leone had easily the worst of it. The Commissioner of Police, Bill Syer, and the head of the CID, Bernard Nealon, could not have been more co-operative and, from Sir Percy down, we were deeply grateful for their attitude.

As we have lately seen, the situation in that unfortunate territory is still far from good, though many of IDSO's recommendations for improving security have been gradually implemented. The permission granted by the Sierra Leone government to the Diamond Corporation to set up diamond buying posts in the vast diamondiferous areas of swamp and jungle in the interior has completely altered the legal and commercial basis of diamond mining and dealing. The basic issue now resolves itself into a straight commercial fight between the Diamond Corporation on the one hand and the IDB on the other. The winner will be whichever side captures the goodwill and output of the thousands of recently legalized African diggers. The IDB have the advantage of being able to fix their prices without taking into account export duty and, in some cases, they are backed by unlimited resources from behind the Iron Curtain. The Diamond Corporation on the other hand has the advantage of official government support, stable prices and, I hope by this time, adequate deterrent measures against smuggling across the Liberian frontier.

Already a very substantial proportion of the illegal traffic has been diverted into the official channels provided by the Diamond Corporation, but the commercial battle is not likely to be decided within a month or a year.

Ian Fleming describes how the Diamond Corporation of Sierra Leone, under the chairmanship of Philip Oppenheimer, has set about its task with tremendous energy and enthusiasm. The Government of Sierra Leone is equally determined to clear out – and keep out – the illegal immigrants from neighbouring French territory who are battening on Sierra Leone. Similarly the thousands of Syrian and European dealers who have acted as middlemen in the past will be obliged to jump off the fence between legality and illegality if they wish to continue either living in or visiting Sierra Leone. The Governor of Sierra Leone recently stated that one dealer alone had sold diamonds to the value of £80,000 to the Diamond Corporation and to the value of £240,000 to the illegal dealers. This man is notorious and it is a pity that his name, like many others, must for the time being be suppressed.

I will end with two general comments on this book.

First, Ian Fleming has adopted the convenient literary device of making one individual, myself, the chief and omniscient operator for IDSO, but I should make it quite clear that the IDSO was a team whose success, such as it was, should be credited to Sir Percy Sillitoe and to the Organization as a whole.

Secondly, I would be the first to admit that our work was by no means completed. Today there are still dotted round the world powerful criminals living beneath a cloak of sunny respectability in an affluence which still comes from diamonds smuggled out of Africa.

These men will hear of this book and they will read it, out of fear or vanity, to see if their activities have been revealed or their names are mentioned.

A word of warning to these far from gentle readers. It is most unlikely that the name of any one of them was not on the files of IDSO in London or Johannesburg; and, though

IDSO itself has been disbanded, 'international diamond security' is not a transient organization, but a permanent function of the police and the Customs men.

'JOHN BLAIZE'

1

THE MILLION-CARAT
NETWORK

IF YOU WRITE SPY THRILLERS YOU ARE APT TO HAVE AN interesting postbag. One day in April 1957 I had just answered a letter from an expert in unarmed combat writing from a cover address in Mexico City, and I was thanking a fan in Chile, when my telephone rang.

It was a friend. He sounded mysterious. 'You remember that job Sillitoe was on? Well, it's just finished and his chief operator says he'll now tell you what it was all about. He's amused by your books, particularly that diamond-smuggling one. He thinks you'd be able to write his story. He's ready to tell you everything within reason – names, dates, places. I've heard some of it and it's terrific. But you'd have to meet him in Africa – Tangier probably. Can you get away?'

I knew something about Sir Percy Sillitoe's job. When

he retired as head of MI5, De Beers had hired him to break the diamond-smuggling racket. Paragraphs about his goings and comings had leaked into the papers from time to time over the last few years. It seemed that the racket had been losing the Diamond Corporation stones worth more than ten million pounds a year. If this unnamed spy would really talk it would obviously be worth sacrificing my Easter holiday. I asked one or two questions. Would these revelations be made with the blessing of De Beers?

They would not. In that case, were there any security objections to the story being told? My friend was of the opinion that there weren't. I said I would go.

My friend gave me the man's name – John Blaize – which was one of his aliases, and a telephone number, improbably enough in Zululand.

There followed a week of meetings – with an informative friend from Scotland Yard; in my club with a mild little man from Antwerp – and a flurry of cables with Blaize of Zululand. I had tried telephoning him, but was told that he was out trying to photograph a white rhinoceros – another touch of the bizarre. Then I took off by Air France to the Hotel El Minzah in Tangier, to wait until, on the thirteenth of the month, John Blaize would contact me.

I had found out what I could about Blaize – public school and Oxford, Bar examinations and then into the office of the Treasury Solicitor. When war came he joined up as a private in a county regiment, but after his commission he was posted to Military Intelligence, where he had done extremely well and ended up as a lieutenant-colonel. After the war he was tempted into MI5 and had been one of the team which eventually broke the Fuchs case. He had then concentrated on penetrating the Communist underground – an unsavoury and sometimes dangerous job which had taken him round the world. In 1954, Sir Percy Sillitoe, one of whose gifts is knowing really good men, enticed him away with a glittering salary to help on the diamond operation.

After that, for three years, Blaize had gone to earth in Africa, whence his activities had sounded echoes in Beirut, Tangier, Antwerp, Paris, Berlin and even Moscow.

Now the job was done, the main leaks plugged, the final arrests made, and Blaize was on his way out of the shadows and back into the light of day.

Blaize duly turned up on time, and we met in my bedroom at the Minzah.

He was a man of about forty, dressed in the typical uniform of the Englishman abroad – Lovat tweed coat, grey flannel trousers, a dark blue rope-knit sweater, nondescript tie, and rather surprisingly, a fine white silk shirt of which he later confessed he owned twenty-four. He had inconspicuous but attractive good looks. He had dark hair flecked with grey, and shrewd, humorous, slate-coloured eyes that turned up slightly at the corners. His smile was warm and his voice quiet with a hint of hesitation. He spoke always with a diffident authority, and whenever I interrupted he would carefully turn over what I had said before replying.

When he was consulting his notes, he was a don or a scientist – head thrust forward, shoulders a little stooped and sensitive, quiet hands leafing through his scraps of paper, but when he crossed the room he looked like a cricketer going out to bat: gay, confident, adventurous.

He was a typical example of the English 'reluctant hero', and I got to like him enormously.

He was tired when he arrived – with a tiredness that came from more than his journey; and shy. He was also rather nervous about being spotted in Tangier, and during the week we worked together he insisted on our meeting at odd places and at odd times. Then he would unburden himself of his story, verifying dates and facts from untidy scraps of paper.

When he had finished I would get the story down and he would later correct what I had written. It was desperately hard work, but we enjoyed it.

Blaize didn't smoke. At our first meeting, after various preliminaries, he stood at the window looking out across the roses and hibiscus in the famous garden of the Minzah towards the crouching clutter of houses that is the Kasbah. He began hesitantly and took time to get into the narrative. This, with a few of my questions and promptings, is how the story went.

'One day early in '54 my old Chief – he'd just retired – invited me to lunch at his club and asked me if I'd like to leave Military Intelligence and join a team to get after the diamond smugglers. We were to be paid by De Beers – big salaries and all expenses. I was tired of routine and, anyway, the late thirties or early forties are a good time for a man to change his job. Sillitoe was always a good man to work for – he looked after his men and got things done – and from what

I had heard of the Oppenheimers and De Beers, they were solid people, too.

'I spent some sleepless nights. This wasn't going to be as easy or, for that matter, as safe a job as being a Civil Servant – if a fairly exciting Civil Servant. It was going to be rather like going to war again. I said yes, and in August 1954, I sailed for Johannesburg.

'I won't tell you all the background of the diamond story. But you'll have to get hold of a few basic facts to understand how the racket started and how it has grown from the old days of IDB – that's Illicit Diamond Buying – when an occasional native boy on the mineface turned up a stone and put it in his mouth instead of on the conveyor.'

'What was the size of the traffic when you took the job?'

Blaize shrugged his shoulders. 'About ten million pounds a year, give or take a million,' he said. 'That year the President of Interpol announced that ten million pounds' worth were being smuggled out of South Africa alone, and that was only one of the sources. But he was rather off the beam about the Union.

'Personally I wouldn't swear to any figure. Smuggling has grown with the industry. When Cecil Rhodes – he was the first chairman of De Beers, by the way – amalgamated the Kimberley Diamond Mines around 1890, one of the objects was to regulate the working of the diamond deposits and set up a common marketing scheme so that the mines wouldn't undercut each other. The idea was to create a world price for diamonds – a monopoly price, really, like we've heard of in other industries: motor tyres, electric light bulbs, television tubes, and so on. So they set up a buying and selling organization known as "The Diamond Syndicate". This ran all right until, from the turn of the century onwards, a whole series of fabulous new diamond fields was discovered.'

Blaize consulted his notes. 'They found the Premier Mine in 1902 – where the Cullinan and other famous stones came from. Then the South-West Africa alluvial fields in 1908. The Congo deposits in 1913. The Portuguese Angola fields in 1916, the Gold Coast industrial diamond fields in 1919, Lichtenburg in 1926, Namaqualand in 1927. The vast fields in Sierra Leone in 1930 and, last but not least, the famous Williamson Mine in Tanganyika in 1940.

'Early on these new discoveries put a strain on the Rhodes selling machinery, and the Diamond Syndicate more or less collapsed. Half way through the list I have given you, confidence in diamonds disappeared almost overnight. People decided diamonds weren't rare any more, and prices nosedived, helped by price-cutting between the rival mining companies. It nearly bust the diamond trade. But then De Beers, who must have had terrific guts, stepped in again and stopped the rot. The companies decided it was better to hang together than separately. They joined up again, and the old Rhodes Diamond Syndicate was re-created.

'The lesson of non co-operation had been learned and the new deposits in the second half of my list – and the companies that owned them – toed the line until Williamson came along. He stuck out for a time – he's a determined, independent character whose biography ought to be written one day – but in the end he came in too, and today about 90 per cent of all the diamonds dug out of the surface of the world are marketed through a subsidiary of De Beers, the Diamond Trading Company – generally known as the Diamond Corporation – in London. It's as solid as the Pru, and one of London's great broking services – a huge dollar-earner for Britain, which is why, as you'll see when I go on with my story, we had no difficulty in getting support from the highest in the land when we needed it.'

Blaize went back to his notes. 'For the record,' he said, 'these are the companies that have selling contracts with the Diamond Corporation:

PORTUGUESE WEST AFRICA
Companhia de Diamantes de Angola

GOLD COAST
Consolidated African Selection Trust Limited

SIERRA LEONE
Sierra Leone Selection Trust Limited

FRENCH EQUATORIAL AFRICA
Société Guiniéenne de Recherches et d'Exploitations Minières

BELGIAN CONGO
Société Internationale Forestière et Minière du Congo
Société Minière du Beceka

TANGANYIKA
Williamson Diamonds Limited

'That's apart, of course, from the Union and South-West African companies owned by De Beers. Much the same machinery exists for industrial stones as opposed to gem stones. These are handled by Industrial Distributors Ltd., of Johannesburg, which is also one of the De Beers group.

'All right, so it looks a nice tidy monopoly picture. And it would be, if there weren't galloping boom conditions in the diamond industry and if there wasn't a huge unsatisfied demand for gem diamonds as a hedge against the inflation that's going on in every country in the world. As for industrial diamonds, these are used for machine tools, and they're being stockpiled in the armaments race, particularly by America, Russia and China. So the black market price of diamonds has soared in the last ten years, and made almost any risk in thieving and smuggling worth while' – Blaize smiled grimly – 'particularly as prison sentences haven't gone up with the price of diamonds. They're the same today as they were when Rhodes set up shop in Kimberley.

'The machinery for handling *legal* diamonds gives no room for alibis. Every month the Diamond Corporation holds "sights" to which the respectable brokers come. There they buy the stones that are up for sale – three million pounds or more at each "sight" and the whole business is as open as the Stock Exchange. But for every honest merchant who is on the Diamond Corporation's approved list, there are two or three not on the list who are known to accept smuggled diamonds or who are known to be selling diamonds through the Iron Curtain.

'They've been blacklisted by the Diamond Corporation.

They've set up their own machinery in Antwerp and Beirut and other places, and they pay the Diamond Corporation prices, and more at times, for the flood of smuggled stones looking for a market. They're receivers of stolen goods in a big way, but the countries where they operate don't care, so long as they take a cut in taxes and import licences and so on, on the way.

'And, anyway, there's a great deal of jealousy in every country interested in diamonds, not excluding America, because London has this monopoly market in the stones.

'As I said, it's a huge trade, and immensely valuable. In 1953, for instance, just before I signed on, sales of legitimate stones alone amounted to sixty-one million pounds. They are around seventy million pounds today. But the black market grew with the white, and De Beers simply had to try to cut it down, both as a service to the various countries and companies involved in the Diamond Corporation, as a natural commercial operation against a competitor and – and this is not quite so incidental as you might imagine – as a patriotic duty: to stop this huge gun-running operation through the Iron Curtain, because industrial diamonds are one of the sinews of armaments.

'So you see, it's gone a long way from the black man slipping a diamond into his mouth and selling it to a pawnbroker in Jo'burg for a few pounds. Today, the I D B operator who buys from the black thief or, more likely, from the respectable European official, can be certain of getting a really good guaranteed price for his stone. Just to give you an idea, the price of a pure blue-white polished gem stone of only one carat has come up from £70 in 1929 to £230 today.

'That's what's made the traffic really worthwhile. I remember Sillitoe saying to me that one of the first questions he had asked Sir Ernest Oppenheimer was: "How far up do you want me to go?" You see, there are fortunes involved for everyone all along the legitimate diamond channels right up to the moment when the merchant at the monthly sights nods his head and signs his cheque. Whatever your salary is, you have to be a good man to turn down the chance of picking up twenty thousand pounds or even a hundred thousand pounds at one swoop, particularly since you only face a small prison sentence if you get caught.'

'But surely there must be machinery for stopping that sort of thing – security checks of all sorts, X-rays and so forth?'

Blaize smiled sourly. 'You'd *think* so,' he said, 'but when we started on the job we were amazed to find how few white men had to go through security. I suppose it was considered undignified to do much about the whites. A lot of that's changed now, but you'd be surprised the snags there are even in a check like X-rays.

'You see, you can't go on X-raying men, even if they're black, again and again. They get loaded with gamma rays. For instance, in places like Kimberley, where most of the European miners go back to their homes every day, if you X-rayed them every time they left the mine they'd die like flies. All you can do is to have an occasional spot check and make the men *think* you're X-raying them when sometimes you're not.

'We had a couple of bright ideas. First we suggested to

the Medical Department of De Beers that an X-ray might be developed powerful enough to show up hidden diamonds but without transmitting too much gamma rays. The company's top doctors, Van Blommestein and Birt, went to America and Holland and found that a machine could be built which would allow a man to be examined for diamonds up to twice a week. They're going ahead with that.

'Then I went to an old friend on the Security Staff at Harwell and asked him if one could radio-activate diamonds and trace them with a Geiger counter. He talked to the atom scientists, but they said you couldn't radio-activate diamonds because they were made of pure carbon. Luckily, the Diamond Research lab. in Jo'burg had been working along the same lines, and they'd invented a way of "labelling" diamonds by painting them with an invisible radio-activated element. This made it possible to plant "labelled" diamonds underground or in the recovery plant to test the honesty of the men. If the labelled diamonds turn up in the day's production at the sort-house, well and good. But if someone picks one up and tries to smuggle it through the turnstiles, a sort of Geiger counter sets off an alarm bell.

'Mark you,' Blaize shrugged his shoulders philosophically, 'these sort of gimmicks are most useful against the coloured workers. Sort of White Man's Magic. But they all help. Just like an occasional flight by helicopter over big mining areas, and setting up television cameras, real ones and dummies, at various points in the plant. These things frighten the small man, but they don't frighten the big ones. The big ones have their own planes for landing in the bush – probably even frogmen for swimming up rivers.

'It's the usual battle of wits between the cops and the robbers. Nowadays, the smugglers are so big and rich that they can spend almost as much money on getting hold of illegal diamonds as the mining companies spend taking legal ones out of the ground.'

'But who are these big people? I still don't get the picture of ten million pounds' worth of diamonds getting smuggled every year. It's a huge operation. Where are they actually smuggled from and to?'

Blaize said, 'I'll tell you about the people as we come to them. As for the smuggling channels' – he searched among his papers – 'here's a copy of a map we drew up showing the principal routes to places all over the world. It'll only give you a rough idea, and it's only part of the story, but you can follow it as I tell you some of the case histories that came up at places like these' – and he took his pencil and jabbed it down from place to place across the map.

'When we got to Jo'burg the first thing to do was to set up an intelligence network which would penetrate this underground railway round the world, and as time went on we gradually got all the junctions covered.' Blaize chuckled. 'We tried to keep out of the limelight, but' – he handed me a crumpled cutting from the *Rand Daily Mail* – 'this sort of thing didn't help much. Anyway, Johannesburg was to be our headquarters, and we set up branch offices at Kimberley, Freetown, Antwerp, Paris and London. Apart from Sir Percy Sillitoe and myself, we had six other Chief Agents. You can't publish their names, but I can tell you that

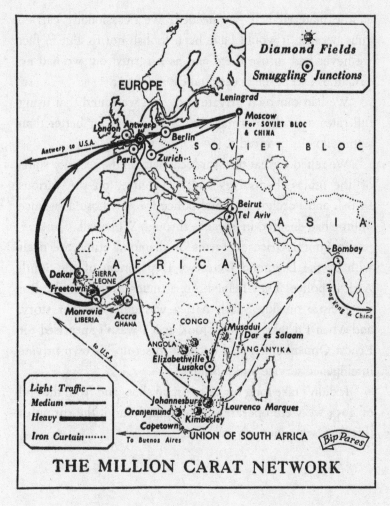

THE MILLION CARAT NETWORK

they were all British with first-class backgrounds in intelligence and security work, and they were all good men.

'It was a happy team and a tough one. We called ourselves IDSO – International Diamond Security Organization. We had an admirable girl to look after our central records and all the material help we needed. We occasionally carried guns because it would have been foolish not to, but in fact we never had to use them and as it turned out we had no casualties except the occasional case of fever.

'We had our own private code and we found that using full rates over the normal cable system was far better than setting up our own radio.

'We relied a great deal for local help on the security staffs of the mines themselves and, of course, on the various British and Foreign Colonial police forces whose assistance Sillitoe had ensured in advance through Whitehall.

'In South Africa all forms of diamond crime are dealt with by the Diamond Detective Department of the South African police. They helped too, as much as they could. But the picture outside South Africa was quite another story, and when I'd taken a good look at it I wasn't surprised Sir Ernest Oppenheimer had decided to set up his own private intelligence service under Sillitoe.

'It didn't take long for us to set up shop, and from the end of 1954 we were operating continuously until the spring of this year, when our job was done.'

2

THE GEM BEACH

DURING THE NIGHT I HAD BEEN THINKING ABOUT Blaize and wondering why he had decided to tell his story. Spies are trained to keep their mouths shut and they don't often lose the habit. That's why true spy stories are extremely rare, and personally I have never seen one in print that rang completely true. Even in fiction there is very little good spy literature. There is something in the subject that leads to exaggeration, and the literary framework of 'a beginning and a middle and an end' doesn't belong to good spy writing, which should be full of loose ends and drabness and ultimate despair. Perhaps only Somerset Maugham and Graham Greene and Eric Ambler have caught the squalor and greyness of the Secret Service.

After a good night's rest some of the tension had gone from the corners of Blaize's mouth and eyes. He diffidently suggested that we should meet somewhere else: 'I'd like to see as much of Tangier as I can while I'm here.'

So we went to the main café, the Café de Paris. The levanter was blowing and it was cold and miserable. We sat in a corner indoors and ordered *espressos,* which we sipped and then forgot.

I asked him why he was telling his story, and whether there weren't any security objections.

Blaize had obviously given the problem a lot of thought. He ran through his reasons briefly and emphatically.

Information about diamond smuggling did not fall within the Official Secrets Act and no security problem was involved, except in so far as the physical safety of a number of crooks was concerned. In Blaize's view it was in the public interest that a bright light should be cast upon perhaps the biggest racket being operated anywhere in the world. Publicity was a weapon against these people and their methods which had not yet been used. It would certainly assist the South African and other police forces and possibly lead them to further sources of information. And, finally, the IDSO operation had been a good one and there was no reason why, like far greater wartime secrets which have since been revealed, the people concerned should not get their share of credit.

Blaize's case seemed to me solid. He didn't plead it, but stated it, and he obviously had no reservations.

I changed the subject and leading on from our previous talk I asked him what sort of people the smugglers had been.

'Smugglers,' said Blaize, 'are all sorts of people. The most dangerous one is the perfectly respectable European mine official who goes into business for himself. He's got no criminal record, but suddenly he likes the idea of having fifty thousand pounds in the bank and perhaps a Cadillac and a girl-friend in Paris. You haven't anything to go on with a man like that. One day he's honest, and then during the night he suddenly decides to be a crook.

'The most extraordinary thing about the diamond business is that there isn't more smuggling and thieving. The prizes are terrific – you could hide enough diamonds on your naked body to make you rich for life – and the penalties if you're caught are extraordinarily small. Of course, if you're caught you lose your name and get a police dossier, which is never a good idea. Nowadays, you could get on the files not only of your own country and the country where you were caught, but also on to the records of Interpol. That can be a nuisance until you've bought yourself a new identity and a new passport in a place like this' – Blaize waved towards the window.

'There's a place down in the Kasbah where you used to be able to pick up fresh papers. It cost around £50 for a British passport and £20 for an American. Americans – the GI and merchant navy type – regard their passports as a last chunk of money to get them home when all the rest is gone. You could have a few things done to your face by a surgeon and get back into circulation again, but even false passports have to be renewed from time to time, and the whole business is pretty tricky. But there are people hiding everywhere – from the police or from their wives or from some childhood sin they think is more important than it really is. If you walk the streets of any big city you'll probably pass one fugitive in every hour.'

Blaize paused. He said reflectively, 'I wonder, for instance, what's happened to a man called Tim Patterson. I shall call him Tim Patterson because from all accounts he was a likeable chap who just found the temptation too much for him. His real name wouldn't mean anything to you and the last thing I want to do is to throw a man's past in his face unless he's a double-dyed villain. Tim Patterson certainly wasn't that. He'll be getting on with a new life somewhere. Probably doing rather well at something. He was an efficient chap and it was really damned bad luck that he got caught.'

'What happened?'

'Patterson was a prospector – an official one – for De Beers. He must have been in his twenties at the time I'm talking of, which was just before I arrived on the scene. De Beers had appointed him to the CDM, the Consolidated Diamond Mines of South-West Africa. If you look at the map of South Africa and run up the west coast about 200 miles, you'll come to Oranjemund – the mouth of the Orange River. From there up the coastline is the most fabulous diamond field in the world. CDM owns 180 miles of it from the mouth of the Orange River up to Diaz Point, near a little harbour called Luderitz. Behind the coast there are thousands of square miles of barren desert with a mountain range behind it – the most forbidding landscape you can imagine.

'Now I won't say that the beaches on the coastline are solid diamonds, but they're certainly well sprinkled with them, and fine gem stones at that. They're bigger near the mouth of the Orange River, and there's no doubt that over the centuries they've been washing in from some huge deposit under the sea. One day, unless it's been exhausted, some bright chap with the right kind of submarine or diving tender will locate that deposit, and, if he can invent a way of mining under the sea, he'll start digging into his diamond nest-egg. When that happens it's just conceivable that the scarcity value of diamonds will be blown to smithereens and they'll become just another semi-precious stone, like sapphires.

'Even now the production of CDM is fabulous. In '54, when I come into the story, they were raking 55,000 carats a month off that beach. Last year they had stepped it up to over 80,000. That's worth more than the total production of all the De Beers mines in South Africa put together.

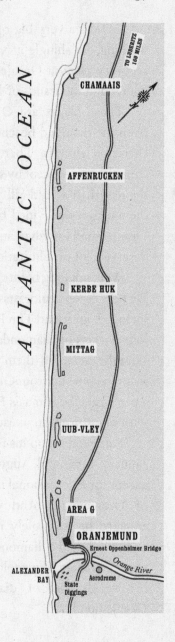

'CDM's a very big operation. The job of screening and washing the shingle at various points up the coast and the recovery plant at Oranjemund need several hundred skilled whites and thousands of blacks.

'These blacks are Ovambos, who are brought to and from the diamond beaches by bus through the desert or by chartered aircraft. There's no other way of getting away from the place except by sea, and you can't walk inland across the desert. It would kill you. So you can *see* that despite all the amenities provided by De Beers in the mining town of Oranjemund for wives and families, the people who live there deserve a lot of admiration.

'Well, not long before I got there, Charles Hallam – one of De Beers's top geologists – and his team of prospectors, which included our friend Tim Patterson, had discovered such fabulous pockets of diamonds up the coast that it was decided to skim the cream off them without waiting for men and equipment to come up from Oranjemund. One of these pockets, at a place called Chamaais Bay, was allotted to young Patterson with one European assistant and a small team of Ovambos.

'Patterson set up his tents just south of the Bay, and from January 1952 until August he was cut off from the world except for an occasional trip down to the comparative luxury of Oranjemund. And when his assistant was otherwise engaged he was solely responsible for counting, weighing and hoarding the diamonds raked off Chamaais Beach. Once a week Hallam, the geologist, paid him a visit and collected his week's haul of diamonds and took them down to Oranjemund.

'So there was Tim Patterson, a young Englishman with a first-class record, who had only been two years in Africa. Everybody liked him, particularly Hallam who went out of his way to mother him. But Patterson was sitting on a fortune, and in the long, lonely nights in his tent he would spread the day's takings on his camp bed and listen to the seals barking on the beach and dream of being rich.

'Nobody knows exactly when Patterson decided to go into business for himself, but I do know that during the months he was at Chamaais more than a million pounds' worth of diamonds went through his hands, and around forty thousand pounds' worth of them stuck to his fingers.

'There was nothing to prevent Patterson helping himself to as many diamonds as he liked, as long as he did so before Hallam turned up in his Land-Rover to weigh and count them. All he had to do was to put some aside when his assistant wasn't looking and think of a way of getting them back to civilization.

'We know that Patterson thought of three ways of getting his stones out. When the time came for him to go on leave he would go down to Oranjemund and there go through the complete CDM security check, which in the case of CDM meant an X-ray examination of every human being, animal and article going through the high wire fence.

'Patterson dismissed from his mind any way of dodging the security controls by trying to beat the X-rays, though he did think of trying to bribe a radiographer. He turned down the idea. It was too risky and Patterson, who was the sort of lone operator I told you about – the ones that are the most difficult to catch – wanted to avoid having obligations to anyone else. He also wanted to get out all his stones and not have to pay a quarter or half of the proceeds to an accomplice.

'Next he thought to take a Land-Rover and, on the excuse of hunting, drive it through the desert to an unpatrolled section of the border and bury the diamonds in the sand near one of the boundary beacons. And come back and collect them when he had reached the outside world.

'But this wouldn't be any good either. It would mean several days away from Chamaais Bay, and in the waterless desert the tracks of the Land-Rover would be evidence against him for years.

'So it had to be some trick to do with the coastline, and that was the way he chose. He would hide his diamond hoard near one of the beaches and come back to the coast by plane or boat. It would mean paying a fat price to a pilot, but probably a few hundred pounds would be enough.

'Once Patterson's mind was made up he started building up his secret stock of diamonds in a canister which he kept buried in the sand under his tent, and in due course, on August 8th, 1952, he went down to Oranjemund and was given a series of farewell parties before he went through his security checks and took the plane off to Johannesburg for the annual leave from which he had no intention of returning. There would be no more hard lying in a tent for Tim Patterson. He would be rich!

'On November 25th Patterson resigned, and he cour-teously wrote to his friend Hallam to say that he would not be coming back to CDM. Hallam and his friends at Oranjemund were sorry. They had all taken to Patterson.'

Blaize paused. He shuffled through his papers and extracted a typewritten sheet. He said, 'For this part of the story I can't do better than read from my notes of the case. I took these down from Piet Willers, who was CDM's Chief Security Officer. He was an efficient and most likeable chap. Although it's nothing to do with the story, he got the job by an extraordinary fluke. The previous Security Chief had been killed by an ostrich. He'd been driving through the desert when one of a flock of ostriches panicked and rushed blindly at his Land-Rover. One of the bird's feet went through the open window, and the central claw stabbed the man through the heart.' Blaize shrugged his shoulders. 'However, this is what his successor, Piet Willers, told me.'

'On Sunday, December 21st, 1952, at 2:30 p.m., Protection Officer du Raan and Prospector Katze came down to my house in Oranjemund, bringing with them T. S. Patterson, the ex-prospector, and a man named "Blake", said to be a pilot. Katze, who was Overseer at the Mining Camp south of Chamaais Bay, informed me that Blake and Patterson had arrived on foot at his camp at 10:30 a.m. on the same day, stating their plane had forced-landed in the neighbourhood of Chamaais Bay.

'I proceeded to interrogate Blake, and he informed me that he and Patterson had left Luderitz by plane at 6:10 a.m., on the same day. His aircraft, an Auster Autocrat, had no wireless, and he had to fly low along the coast to keep his bearings and contacts with the ground. He eventually got in under the fog, which became so low that it clamped down on him, as he expressed it, and he was forced to land.

'I felt suspicious about this story, and asked Blake why he should not fly through the fog or turn inland and fly outside the fog, which Patterson must have known from his experience of living at Chamaais Bay never extended farther than three to five miles inland. Blake replied that he was flying lower than forty feet and could not get out between the hills, nor could he attempt climbing as he was unaware of the height of the fog.

'I then questioned Katze about the weather conditions that morning at his mining camp and along the sea towards Chamaais Bay. He informed me that there was very little fog low down on the sea, and added that the pilot had also told him that he had to make a forced landing owing to engine trouble.

'After I had warned Blake and Patterson that we were going to investigate the circumstances of their forced landing, I had them removed to the local police quarters at Oranjemund. I also made a report to Mr. Louwrens, the General manager.' Blaize shook his head sadly.

'Poor chap. He'd come unstuck. The first thing Louwrens did was to send a certain Davis, one of his air mechanics, up to have a look at the crashed aircraft with Willers. They drove all night and found the plane just as dawn was breaking. It had crashed a few yards from the sea. That was the true part of Patterson's story but the tracks told another tale.

'First of all, there were two clear wheel tracks, showing

that the plane had made a perfect landing, from south-west to north-east. Two men had got out of the plane, one wearing gym shoes. They had walked together along the beach and then turned and come back again and got into the plane and turned it round so that it faced south-west. Then another lot of tracks showed that the plane had started down the beach on its takeoff, but just at the moment when it was going to get airborne the left wheel hit a rock. Then both wheels struck, and the plane had crash-landed another 150 yards farther on among the rocks.

'The pilot must have done a good job and they were lucky not to have been killed. As it was one of the wings, and the under-carriage and the propeller, had been smashed, but unfortunately for Patterson's story the engine was intact, and when they tested it a few days later with a new propeller, there was nothing wrong with it.

'While Patterson sat in jail the case was handed over to the Diamond Detective Department, and a certain Sergeant Cilliers took over. He was faced with the problem that no diamonds had been found on either of the men or their aircraft, and the only crime the men could be charged with was trespass.

'But then inquiries were made at Luderitz and it was found that Patterson had bought a forty-foot fishing boat and had hired a skipper, who had no idea what he was wanted for but who knew the coast, to sail him down to Capetown – an unlikely trip to make. It had obviously been an alternative plan which Patterson had dropped in favour of the aircraft.

'On Christmas Eve Patterson and the pilot, faced with

all the evidence, owned up. They had come to pick up Patterson's diamonds, and when Sergeant Cilliers took Patterson under guard to the beach Patterson showed him the canister under a rock where he had hidden it after the plane had crashed. Inside there were 1400 diamonds of various sizes, weighing 2276 carats. They would have been worth about £40,000.

'Poor Patterson! He and the pilot were tried at Luderitz. They got them under the Diamond Industry Protection Proclamation of 1939. Patterson got nine months' hard labour and Blake got six. Not much. That's what I mean about it being well worth the gamble. Patterson will have been out for more than three years. I wonder what he's doing now. I'm rather sorry for him, really. It was a good scheme and it nearly came off, and I certainly wouldn't like to find myself in reach of a million pounds of somebody else's money.'

I said, 'With all those diamonds to be found on the beach I wonder they don't have a smuggling case every week.'

'That's what I thought when I got there,' said Blaize. 'They had just got over another case when I arrived. It was a smaller business, but fairly typical. Like to hear about it?'

'Yes.'

'There was a man working in the stores at Oranjemund. He was a respectable chap whom I'll call de Graaf. Quite a pillar of the local rugger club. He had a friend called Andries Coetzee, one of the duty radiographers on the Security Staff. One evening early in January 1954 de Graaf invited Coetzee and his wife to his house for a drink. There was nothing suspicious in this. In these mining townships there's an endless round of visits between the houses, and anyway the two knew each other well.

'After a certain amount of the usual chitchat and a drink or two de Graaf rather cryptically asked Coetzee to come into his bedroom as he wanted to "talk business". Coetzee couldn't imagine what sort of "business" there was to discuss, but he went into the bedroom and asked what it was all about. De Graaf simply said, "Well, if you are afraid, say so." When Coetzee looked dumb, de Graaf, who must have been a theatrical sort of chap as well as rather crazy, went to the wardrobe and produced a jar of Vaseline, which he brought back and raised significantly in front of Coetzee's blank eyes. He then, still without saying anything, unscrewed the top and dug his finger into the Vaseline and extracted a big diamond. Coetzee began to understand.

'De Graaf then took out two more diamonds and held the sticky stones out in his hand. He propositioned Coetzee to take the stones out of the compound. It would be easy for Coetzee. He was a trusted man and above suspicion. De Graaf said he had another diamond hidden in the garden. He would pay Coetzee a quarter of the value of the four stones.

'Coetzee was bowled over by this proposition, particularly as it came from de Graaf, whom he'd thought of up till then only as a pleasant fellow and a good rugger player. Coetzee said all right, he would do the job. All he asked was that de Graaf should tell him which day he wanted the deed done. Then they went back to Mrs. Coetzee in the living-room.

'The next morning Coetzee went straight to the General Manager, and from that moment all his dealings with de Graaf were controlled by Piet Willers, the Security Officer, and Sergeant Cilliers of the Diamond Detectives.

'Nothing happened for a fortnight, then de Graaf had another talk with Coetzee and asked if he was really ready to go through with his end of the job. Coetzee said that he felt perfectly happy about the whole business – which he probably did, as it was going to mean promotion for him – and de Graaf handed over the four diamonds and told him to keep them for the time being. They were later found to weigh 104 carats and were valued at over £6000.

'Meanwhile the security people were wondering how the devil de Graaf, who worked in the stores, could have got hold of the diamonds. Obviously he had accomplices and Coetzee was briefed to try and find out who they were. A few days later, de Graaf buttonholed Coetzee and produced another thirty-seven small diamonds weighing 26 carats. He now thought that he had Coetzee involved up to his neck in the business, and treated him as his partner in crime.

'In the course of conversation Coetzee discovered that de Graaf had three Europeans and two Ovambos collecting for him. A month later de Graaf handed over another sixteen diamonds weighing 37 carats, and revealed the names of his accomplices.

'The Diamond Detectives held their hand, and at the end of March de Graaf put in his resignation and went and saw Coetzee to make his final arrangements, which were simple. As soon as de Graaf had been searched and X-rayed and was free to leave for the outside world, Coetzee in the X-ray Department was to slip him the bag of diamonds, and de Graaf would take the company bus across the Orange River to freedom.

'All went well, and de Graaf was on his way to the bus with a fortune in his pocket when the detectives pounced. The smuggler put up a fight, but was finally overcome and carried off to jail. De Graaf got three years' hard labour, and his chief accomplice two years. The rest of the dozen or so crooks were sacked and blacklisted. Coetzee got his promotion.'

Blaize concluded, 'A typical, sordid little case involving a lot of small crooks and one honest man. Not very interesting, really, but you get a sort of breath of the compound life of drinks and rugger and "good chaps", one of whom had something besides lint and liniment stashed away in the medicine cabinet in his tidy little bungalow.'

3

THE DIAMOND DETECTIVES

T HE NEXT DAY WE WENT FOR A WALK THROUGH THE Kasbah to the Sultan's Palace, where we were picked up by an extremely young guide and forced to say 'How interesting!' at intervals for about half an hour's sightseeing. We were delighted when, in accordance with tradition, the guide offered us his sister at the end of the tour, but we chastely retired to a roof café overlooking the beautiful crescent of Tangier Bay and ordered mint tea.

I was getting to know Blaize. There are many types of secret agent, from the drab 'private eye' soaked in alcohol and nicotine who spies on wives and husbands and lovers, to the top professionals. The finest craftsman is a man like Alexander Foote, who worked all through the war for the Russians and became their top man in Switzerland. Foote, besides being an expert wireless operator, was a careful, dedicated man who worked for a cause and not for money. He came over to England after the war and settled down quietly to working for the Ministry of Agriculture and Fisheries. He died last year, I heard.

Then there are the colourful spies like Sorge, the brilliant, luxury-loving German who worked for Russia in Tokio, and girls like Christine Granville who was murdered by a love-crazed ship's steward in a Kensington hotel in March 1952, after a fabulous record in wartime espionage for which she earned the George Medal.

But Blaize, like all Britain's best secret agents, belonged to none of these categories. He had common sense, a passion for accuracy and a knowledge of men and how to use them which would have brought him to the top of, for instance, the Civil Service. But he also had a taste for adventure and a romantic streak which in the Civil Service would have been sublimated into mountain climbing and amateur theatricals.

That morning, as we watched the levanter corral the white horses into the Bay of Tangier, he gave me the details of the 'Desmond' case, and I think his preliminary remarks illustrate the down-to-earth, commonsense qualities of the man.

Blaize said: 'I'm afraid I'm not giving you much of a picture of my day-to-day life chasing after smugglers. After a bit it became rather dull; a hard grind of air trips round the various mines all over Africa, making myself pleasant to the local big brass; keeping my eyes open and trying to make it seem that my suggestions for improving security had been made by the man I was talking to and not by me.

'You can imagine that IDSO wasn't very popular. We were a private army and we were from London. On the other hand we'd got absolute carte blanche from Sir Ernest Oppenheimer himself, and it would be wise to co-operate with us – or at least to seem to do so.

'It was rather like during the War, when private armies sprang up and had their day until they made a mistake and were disbanded or swallowed up by the Intelligence "Establishment" who thought they ought to have a monopoly. You'll remember what it was like, particularly at the beginning, when two or three separate teams were all plotting to blow up the Iron Gates on the Danube for instance. And then later, in Yugoslavia, when rival gangs were dropping arms to Mihailovic and the Reds. Then they formed SOE to try to straighten things out, and SOE found themselves up against the Secret Service and Naval Intelligence, OSS, MEW, G2 and all the others.

'Why, only the other day you got much the same sort of picture from Crabb's disastrous frogman exploit. That was a "private army" job that should have been handled – if it was handled at all – by the Navy, who know infinitely more about frogmen than any Secret Service. You'll remember how that one blew up in everybody's face.

'Well, IDSO must have had the same sort of look about it to the regular De Beers security staffs and to the Diamond Detective Department in Kimberley, and heat was generated all over the place. A lot of my job consisted of being tactful and saying "After you, Alphonse" to self-important officials all over Africa.

'And, of course, wires got pretty badly crossed some-times. A good deal of my work consisted of handling double agents – finding an underground smuggling channel and putting a spy in at one end in the hopes that he'd work his way up it till he got to the top.'

Blaize smiled – 'Rather like that book you wrote last year, but the girls don't come quite so pretty around the diamond fields. Anyway, right at the beginning a very promising double-agent spiel ended in the most idiotic shambles.

'It involved a bright, good-looking young man called "Desmond". He's going straight now. That was the code name we gave him at the time, and I'll have to use code names for some of the other performers as they haven't all been rounded up yet.

'This chap came from a very good South African family, but he went wrong, and in 1951 he got a two-year sentence for conspiracy to defraud. In prison, a likeable rascal called Sammy Silberstein took a shine to him. Sammy's a well-known Jew from Jo'burg. He was doing time for illegal possession.

'Well, he got hold of Desmond and told him there were fortunes to be picked up in IDB. He said that he'd been buying Kimberley stones for twenty years, but that they'd got him so often that if he made another mistake he might easily get "life". He told Desmond that Desmond was just the man to act as his front. He'd got the appearance and the manners and the influential friends.

'To cut a long story short, by the time Desmond came out in October '53, they were firm friends, and Desmond had agreed to look out for a safe market in Europe for Sammy's stones. Sammy said that a parcel was already waiting for disposal, and that it was worth forty thousand pounds. A regular supply was assured.

'Desmond had no intention of doing what Sammy wanted. He had decided to go straight. After prison he flew straight to England and joined his wife and spent the next few months looking for a job. Then, just after he'd got some sort of job as a salesman, he saw in the papers that Sillitoe had been taken on by De Beers to fight the smuggling racket.

'Desmond was interested. He saw a chance to redeem his past and perhaps get a chit from Sillitoe which might lead to a better job than being a commercial traveller. He talked things over with his wife — she must have been a good girl, by the way; she'd stood by Desmond all through his troubles — and finally wrote to Sillitoe and went to see him, and told him the whole story.

'Sillitoe liked the look of Desmond and believed him, but IDSO was just beginning, and we were all on our best behaviour vis-a-vis the South African police, so Sillitoe decided to hand the case over to the Diamond Detective Department in Kimberley.

'Sillitoe saw Brigadier Rademeyer, the South African Deputy Commissioner of Police, and he agreed to use Desmond's services, on condition that IDSO paid all Desmond's expenses, including air fares and hotel bills, and gave Desmond part of the value of any diamonds that might be recovered as a result of the operation.'

Blaize smiled. 'Pretty stiff terms, but as I said, we didn't want to step on any corns at this stage of IDSO's career. Desmond flew out and I handed him over to become a police agent, acting under the instructions of Captain van der Westhuisen, who was head of the Diamond Detective Department in Kimberley.

'Well, the police briefed Desmond to contact Sammy Silberstein, who was out of jail by then. Desmond had no difficulty. Sammy owned a garage in Kimberley, and he was delighted to see Desmond again. The only trouble was that Sammy's friends thought Sammy talked too much – which he certainly did – and he'd been demoted from the head of his old IDB ring. Another man had taken over. He was a shrewd and very cautious operator, whom I'll call "X". And X was a very different kettle of fish from Sammy Silberstein. He at once refused to have anything to do with Desmond, in spite of Sammy's personal introduction, and he also gave Sammy strict orders that he wasn't to do any business with Desmond without X's approval. Desmond was tough. He recognized X as a very dangerous man, but he persevered, and finally, after Desmond had spent several weeks hanging around the garage making friends with the rest of the ring, X thawed and said he'd do a deal with Desmond if the prices were right.

'Desmond's story was that he'd got this market in London, and that he was now in Africa looking for stones. X said vaguely that he knew somebody who might know where there was a "parcel" of Fine White and Cape gems, but before there was any question of getting any nearer this parcel he must know what prices Desmond's principals would pay.

'Desmond went through the motions of cabling to London, and in due course handed X a cable that went like this:

FINE WHITE AND WHITE STONES OF GOOD QUALITY –
BETWEEN £17 10S PER CARAT FOR ONE CARATERS
TO £60 PER CARAT FOR FIVE CARATERS; £90 PER
CARAT FOR TEN CARATERS AND £120 PER CARAT FOR
FOURTEEN CARATERS.

CAPE STONES BETWEEN £10 PER CARAT FOR ONE
CARATERS TO £40 PER CARAT FOR TEN CARATERS.

'X said he was satisfied, and it looked to Desmond as if he'd got X in the bag.

'Not so. The Diamond Detective Department said that another witness would have to be present when the deed was done and the transaction took place. They thought up a gimmick which should have worked but didn't, to get a policeman into the act. You see, Desmond had never pretended to know anything about diamonds, and X knew he'd no idea of values. At the same time, obviously, one of Desmond's principals would have to be present when the stones were handed over and the money paid if both sides agreed on a valuation. This would be an expert job.

'So Desmond was told to tell X that his chief was so interested that he himself would fly over from London to complete the deal.

'Typically, X's suspicions were immediately aroused. Like all really good crooks, although he couldn't see it, he smelt the trap.

'Desmond bluffed him out of his suspicions. Somebody would have to agree the values. His people weren't going to buy stones unseen. Anyway, the whole deal depended on mutual trust, and if X really wanted a market for his stones, this was no way to go on.

'But X was adamant, and there was a period of deadlock. This provided a useful breathing space for the Diamond Detectives to find their idea of the right man to pose as Desmond's principal and an expert diamond valuer. They found a South African police officer of English origin – a very rare bird these days – with only a faint South African accent, and they came to me and asked me to fix him up for a course of training by the Diamond Corporation in valuing stones. They also requested IDSO to pay this man's expenses in London while he was learning about diamonds.

'Again we wanted to be co-operative, and we agreed, and the man, whom we hadn't seen but knew as "Charlie", went to London and by November he'd learned all he could absorb. Desmond went back to X and got him interested again, and X finally agreed that he would meet Desmond's principal in Kimberley.

'I took the precaution of going to Jo'burg to have a look at Desmond's "principal" when he stepped off the plane from London, and I was horrified to find that he was completely miscast for the role of a high-powered diamond dealer with a bottomless purse. I told the Diamond Detectives that their man couldn't possibly be expected to fool X unless his status was whittled down. They agreed, and Desmond was briefed to tell X that his principal had gone sick and was sending a junior valuer in his place.

'I don't know how X reacted to this further change of plan, but it can't have improved his confidence in Desmond, and I was certain in my mind that the whole operation was going sour.

'However, the situation was out of our hands and the machine slowly ground on towards disaster.

'The "junior valuer", his big policeman's boots showing at the ends of his trousers, met Desmond in Kimberley, and I paid £50,000 into an account at the Standard Bank so that if all went well the packet of stones could be paid for.

'They met – the two police spies and the formidable X. X played his cards beautifully. No mention was made of any packet of diamonds. Instead, X drew the "junior valuer" into a highly technical discussion of diamond values. Charlie survived the first part of this well enough, but later allowed himself to be drawn deeper and deeper into technicalities, in which he floundered hopelessly. When his ignorance had been finally revealed, X slapped him cheerfully on the back, told him he was a nice chap but knew nothing about diamonds, and wished him good afternoon. And that was that.

'But all was not necessarily lost. As I said, Desmond was a tough chap and he was determined to get as many of the gang into the bag as he could, even if he couldn't get the top man, and he switched his attention back to Sammy Silberstein and the smaller fry.

'Without consulting X, Sammy arranged a meeting at his garage to which he told Desmond he would invite plenty of sellers with real goods to offer. Sammy was attracted by the £50,000 which Desmond told him was waiting to buy gems in the Standard Bank, and he didn't like the idea of the "junior valuer" closing his account and going back to London without spending any of it.

'This would have been the moment for the Diamond Detectives to raid the garage. Instead, they did nothing. In any case, Fate was tired of Desmond's game and had decided to send him packing.

'When Desmond and his "valuer" came into the garage Charlie recognized among the guests a certain "Johnny", who had been a fellow prisoner of Desmond's in jail. And unfortunately, Johnny was a man Charlie had got sentenced to four years' imprisonment for robbery.

'Desmond and his "valuer" withdrew and conferred. They decided that discretion was the better part of valour. Johnny would certainly beat up the "valuer", and probably both of them, and anyway, by now Desmond was getting thoroughly fed up with the whole business.

'But he cleaned the case up nicely, and left it all neat and tidy for the police to continue with if they wanted. He went to Jo'burg and called up Sammy and said he'd been stopped and searched on his way to the garage and was lucky to have got away. He accused Sammy of being a police informer, and said he'd have nothing more to do with him. Sammy swore that he was Desmond's best friend, and begged him to stay in Jo'burg so that he could prove his innocence with a big packet of stones. Desmond said that he was running no more risks and slammed down the receiver.'

Blaize sighed. 'So that was that. I met Desmond that night

and he told me the whole story – and left the next day for London. We paid him a bonus for his services, and I hope he's got a good job today. He deserves one.

'As it turned out, the operation wasn't a total loss. Desmond had picked up a lot of information for the police, and later they trapped Johnny and another of Sammy's friends. Desmond had got the names of a number of the men at the mines who were stealing, and these people were sacked and blacklisted. So the Diamond Detectives got quite a lot of feathers in their cap.

'But we weren't impressed. X was still at liberty, and he was the big operator who really mattered. However, we'd learned one thing, and that was that we had somehow to establish closer co-operation with the Diamond Detective Department.

'Of course, you can see for yourself what the big mistake was in this case. It was that the Diamond Detectives had insisted on having their own man to be the witness, and not a *real* valuer whom the Diamond Corporation would have been happy to fly out from London.

'If we had worked more closely together, between us we could have brought off a real coup. As it was there was the sort of tug-of-war between rival organizations that I was talking about earlier. The result was that we both made fools of ourselves.'

I asked if the relationship between the South African police and IDSO had got better after the initial suspicion had worn off.

Blaize said: 'In some respects. Colonel Grobeler of the

Johannesburg Division could not have been a nicer man to deal with. I suspect that the trouble lay in Pretoria. I was once told by a retired Captain of the CID, who was in a position to know, that we were suspected of really being agents of the British Government and that our chief mission was to spy on the South African police. According to this CID chap, files had been opened for each member of IDSO in Pretoria and it was quite likely that we ourselves were being watched!

'No, I can hardly call our relationship a bed of roses, even at the end, but it was largely a question of individuals. Just to give you an instance, whenever there was a vacancy on one of the mine security staffs De Beers automatically accepted the custom that it should be filled by a retired member of the South African police – subject, of course, to the man having a top level recommendation.

'On one of these occasions Pretoria sold them a real pup. At first sight he seemed far too boastful and dogmatic a character to make a good security officer. However, we couldn't offend Pretoria out of hand and decided to give him a chance. I sent him up to Tanganyika to work directly under the CID there on a short term operation to get a line on some smugglers we were after. The result was a shambles. Pretoria's special selection at once let down the Tanganyika police by giving away his undercover job to the very IDB ring he was meant to be penetrating, and then sat back and used our funds betting unsuccessfully with the local bookmakers.

'He left a trail of bad debts and bouncing cheques and when the pace got too hot for him, he came back to Jo'burg and pretended to go sick. I went along to interrogate him and he practically threw a fit, ending up by shouting at me: "You English swine, what right have you got to be in this country anyway!"'

Blaize laughed sourly. 'See what I mean? But he wasn't typical. We made plenty of friends in the Union and anyway most of our work was with the British police forces in places like Sierra Leone, Rhodesia, Bechuanaland and Tanganyika. You won't find better policemen than them anywhere in the world.'

4

THE SAFE HOUSE

THE WORLD OF SPIES IS AS FULL OF JARGON AS MOTOR racing or film making, but when Blaize used one of the terms of his trade he did so with irony, making the phrase sound as if it was in quotation marks. Most secret agents are snobbish about their calling. They enjoy 'name-dropping' about cut-outs, postboxes, burnt contacts, double agents, conscious and unconscious agents, de-briefing and the rest. But Blaize regarded the life he was now leaving with healthy scepticism. He had been in it for fifteen years, and he considered that many of its denizens were 'phonies' and much of its products 'bull' – a favourite expression of his.

In all his talks with me Blaize never struck a note that didn't ring true. There were no heroics; successes were strokes of luck and the word 'danger' was never mentioned. He discussed his cases clinically and when, in turning them into prose, I heightened a fact or a situation, he politely but firmly put me right with a mild, 'It wasn't *quite* like that'.

My difficulty was to make him realize that what was humdrum to him was strange and exciting to me. It wasn't easy to clothe the skeleton of his story with flesh, and such background detail as I have been able to achieve was extracted from him during our interminable walks through the Kasbah and in the country round Tangier and over drinks in bars and night-clubs.

We somehow got on to the subject of spy jargon after a round of golf at the grandly named Diplomatic Country Club. Blaize had said his handicap was nine. I also am nine, but Blaize was a far better nine than I, and in fact I didn't win a hole from him. His ball was always straight down the fairway, while I was too often in the impenetrable rough, ablaze with irises and asphodel, which lines the dry watercourses around and over which the course has been constructed.

After the game, as we sat outside the deserted clubhouse sipping gin and tonic, some chance remark of mine started Blaize off about IDSO's 'safe house'.

'Clausewitz's first principle of war,' he said, 'was to have a secure base, and as soon as I and the rest of the team arrived in Johannesburg we set up what's known in spy jargon as a "safe house", well away from our headquarters. This was a flat in the back streets of Johannesburg where we could meet our contacts, particularly the dubious and dangerous ones. We told the Diamond Detective Department that we'd got this place, and said they could use it, too, if they wanted to.

They seemed very grateful because, oddly enough, they had nowhere like this themselves, but I don't think they did in fact ever use it. It wasn't much of a flat. Just a living-room with a few sticks of furniture and a sofa, and an alcove bedroom off it divided from it by a curtain, and a lavatory next door. The only sign of comfort was a sideboard with drinks.'

'Was it wired for sound?'

'No. I had something better than that. A gadget called a Minifon. You can buy them on the open market, but it was actually the Gestapo who invented them. You carry the recorder in your waistcoat pocket or under your armpit, and wires lead down your sleeve to the pick-up, which to all intents and purposes is a wrist-watch. It's one of those tricky gadgets that actually works. It came in pretty useful from time to time.

'Oddly enough, one of the first people to come to the safe house was William Percival Radley – "Tony" Radley. Remember the name? A year later he turned Queen's Evidence in the £200,000 jewel robbery at the house of Harry Oppenheimer. We'd been tipped off by London that a man of this name was believed to have arrived in Nairobi. London suggested that it might be worth keeping an eye on him. We drew a blank with the Kenya police, but then we saw in a Johannesburg paper that a certain Tony Radley was running a dance hall called the 'Palais' on Commissioner Street.

'We were still going very carefully with the South African police, so we followed protocol and told the Diamond Detective Department in Kimberley what we knew of

Radley, and that we thought he might be a good contact for IDSO. The police didn't react to our tip-off, and we went ahead on our own and contacted Radley in the hubbub of juke-box music and taxi-girls at the "Palais". Later, Radley met us at the safe house and seemed willing enough to help, but in fact he had only fag-ends of information on IDB which he tried to make sound important with the typical blarney of that kind of man.

'By early in 1955 we'd got all we could out of Radley and we discarded him. The next time he cropped up was in the Oppenheimer robbery.

'By chance, the other defendant in the Oppenheimer case also turned up about that time. This was Donald Miles, the ex-Palestine policeman and Festival of Britain Security Officer, who was later to be charged with Radley. In a way I feel rather responsible for the trouble he was to get into. He came to see me in July of '55 wanting a job as a mine security officer. He'd had a good war record and had a wad of fine testimonials from his previous jobs. He had just the qualifications we needed, but as luck would have it there were no vacancies and I had to turn him down. Six months later he was charged in connection with the robbery. I'm glad to say he was found innocent.

'But to go back to the safe house. To begin with, we had a regular flow of visitors passed on to us from various sources. They generally came at night – all kinds of people, most of them bogus, and most of them wanting money. Sometimes they had scraps of information for which we paid a pound or two. Sometimes they wanted to work off old scores against an official in one of the mines or a private enemy, and very occasionally there was a gold nugget in the dirt. One of these turned up in February '55.

'It came about like this. In September of '54 a certain character I'll call Kutze had been arrested at Beit Bridge, which is the frontier post on the Limpopo between Southern Rhodesia and the Union. In Kutze's waistcoat pocket was a fine rough diamond of over eight carats, and in November he came up for trial for unlawful possession and was fined £200. The Diamond Trading Company bought the stone. They decided it was alluvial and from West Africa, and that it had probably been peddled right across Africa before being sold to Kutze in Rhodesia. The fact that he'd been convicted was a much more serious blow to the man than his fine or even the loss of his stone. It meant that he was now a marked man in Rhodesia, which was his field of operations, and he complained bitterly about his luck to an old friend called Karl, with whom he'd once been associated.

'Now it happened that Karl had once been a police informer in Kimberley, and he had not forgotten the fat rewards you could get for successful informing. Kutze gave him plenty of ammunition about IDB in Rhodesia, and in February '55 Karl went along to have a chat with Detective Constable Grobbelaar, head of the Johannesburg branch of the Diamond Detectives. Grobbelaar was a first class police-man and when he heard Karl's story, he thought that Karl might get further with IDSO than with the South African police, and he telephoned me and suggested that we should see Karl at the safe house. If you know anything about

Afrikaners you'll know that they are the worst sufferers in the world from verbal diarrhoea. They talk in torrents, and the more they talk, the more intoxicated they are with their own eloquence. When Karl sat down with a drink in his hand in the safe house and started talking, I was smothered in a jabbering cataract of words of which I could only understand about one in ten. Gradually, by banging on the table to stop him and firing questions which required only a "Yes" or a "No", I began to sort out the oral jigsaw puzzle, and in the end the effort was worth while.

'According to Karl, the diamond which Kutze had lost on Beit Bridge was a mere drop in the ocean. The Copperbelt was lousy with IDB smuggled stones. They were being brought in from the Gold and Ivory Coasts, from Williamson's mine in Tanganyika, and from the Belgian Congo, and there was a steady stream of Europeans coming up from the Union to buy these stones from the native runners and make huge profits when they got them back to the cutters in Jo'burg. Karl proposed to use the names and contacts divulged to him by Kutze to penetrate the racket for IDSO.

'I took Karl on with the object of running my own little double-agent spiel on much the same lines that had failed with Desmond. I had to square the South African and the Northern Rhodesian police, and tell them what I intended to do, and I agreed to keep everybody fully informed of progress, and finally it was fixed. Karl would travel up the pipeline into Rhodesia, contact the IDB ring Kutze had told him about, buy diamonds and bring them over the frontier into the Union. There they would be taken from him and sold to the Diamond Corporation, and he could keep any profit he made in exchange for full information on the Rhodesian ring.'

Blaize paused. 'Mark you,' he said, 'at that time I wasn't quite certain where I stood with Karl. The South African police had absolutely nothing against him, but it was a dangerous thing for me to connive in smuggling diamonds from Rhodesia into the Union. I'd persuaded the South African and the Rhodesian police to leave Karl alone, and I was really in the position of making him a licensed smuggler. And the trouble with diamonds is that every stone carries the germ of crime in it. Karl was a perfectly honest man, but what would be the effect on him of buying cheap IDB diamonds with IDSO money and being faced with the chance of making a fortune if he could get them back into the Union without us knowing?

'I thought the position over and finally decided that we wouldn't finance Karl on his first trip, but that he would have to raise a thousand pounds or so through his own resources. This made the picture a little better from our point of view, but it still was anything but watertight. It was in the early days of IDSO, and I kept my fingers crossed.

'I wasn't made any happier by my last meeting with Karl in the safe house before he took the plane for Ndola. He said that Kutze now refused to give him the names of his contacts in Rhodesia. Kutze must have smelt trouble, or perhaps Karl talked too much. It was too late to change my plans, so I gave Karl the name of a man living in Kitwe who had written to IDSO offering to act as an informer. Also, since we were going to pay all Karl's expenses and if the spiel was a failure I didn't want it to be an expensive one, I told Karl to report progress after two weeks, by sending one of three telegrams, according to the situation.

They were:

ONLY SMALL BUSINESS AVAILABLE SO FAR WILL CABLE AGAIN ON . . .

BUSINESS NOT WORTH WHILE RETURNING ON . . .
and

BUSINESS GOOD SALES EXPERT REQUIRED ON . . .

'The last was in case such big stones were turning up that Karl needed an expert valuer.

'Well, Karl flew off for the Copperbelt on March 7th, and on the 18th I got the Number 2 telegram: BUSINESS NOT WORTH WHILE RETURNING ON MARCH 22.

'This seemed too bad to be true. IDB was rife in the Copperbelt, and it was unthinkable that Karl hadn't managed to penetrate the market. My worst suspicions were aroused. I felt sure my double-agent had turned triple, and that he'd spent his whole thousand pounds on cheap stones and would now try to smuggle them under cover of IDSO and make his profit. I talked the position over with the helpful Detective Constable Grobbelaar, and I suggested that Karl should be put through the wringer by the Customs on his arrival. Grobbelaar agreed.

'On March 22nd Karl duly disembarked at the Jan Smuts airport from the Ndola plane, and was impressed to find that he was the first passenger to be selected to pass through the Customs – a distinction usually reserved for VIPs. He must have been struck with the importance and influence of IDSO. His illusions were shattered when he and his suitcase were taken into a separate room and ignominiously and thoroughly searched.

'Karl, highly indignant, addressed himself to a man in plain clothes, complaining of his insulting treatment. The man introduced himself as Sergeant Smith of the Diamond Detective Department. "I thought you'd be here to save me all this!" Karl shouted angrily, and then, with less bravado, "The diamonds are in the handle".

'Stolidly, Smith examined the handle of the suitcase and carefully unstitched the leather to reveal fifty-two diamonds packed in cotton-wool. He then told Karl that the stones would have to be declared. This was done, and the diamonds duly impounded and sealed and left in the possession of the Customs.

'All this while Karl was assuring Smith that the whole matter could be satisfactorily explained, but that he must be brought to me, and in due course Smith escorted him to the safe house and the interrogation began.

'Karl reported that he had arrived in Ndola airport and had hired a taxi to take him the forty miles to his hotel in Kitwe. He at once started talking to the native driver about buying diamonds in the neighbourhood, and the driver had given him the name of another taxi man who he said knew the whole diamond market in the Copperbelt as well as the names of the native runners.

'Karl couldn't believe his luck, and thought that either

the driver was boasting wildly or that IDB was wide open in Rhodesia. In fact, Karl had tumbled on just the right contact, and the other taxi man arranged a series of fruitful meetings. But, according to Karl, although he listened to endless talk and a lot of promises, after ten days in Kitwe he hadn't bought a single diamond, and he had decided to force the issue by sending me his negative telegram and telling his IDB contacts that as there was nothing for him to buy he was packing his bag and leaving in three days.

'The ruse certainly worked, and during the last three days he was deluged with diamonds from Europeans and from native runners coming across the Congo-Rhodesian border.

'In the process of these deals Karl was able to compile a formidable list of names, both of the smuggling network into Rhodesia and of the European pipeline over the frontier into the Union.

'Karl said that the people he'd had to deal with were a pretty grisly crew, steeped in treachery and double-dealing. Not only did they buy the stones from the native runners and sell them to the smugglers from the Union, but they supplemented their profits by informing to the Northern Rhodesian police not only on their competitors, but also on their own customers.'

Blaize added: 'Incidentally, this habit of working for both sides in IDB is an old story, and makes running agents a complicated and risky business. Anyway, Karl had certainly done his stuff, and the only two questions were why he hadn't sent a second telegram cancelling the first when the diamonds began to flow, and why he'd hidden the diamonds in the handle of his suitcase.

'Karl said that there had been no point in sending another telegram as anyway his money had run out. As to the business with the handle of his suitcase, he had expected to be met by the Diamond Detective Department at the Customs, and had only gone to the trouble of hiding the stones in the handle of his suitcase to show how easy it was to fool the Customs. He made no attempt to conceal the stones once he had met Sergeant Smith.

'This sounded fair enough to me and the Diamond Detectives were satisfied. In the end Karl had done very well, and both the Northern Rhodesian police and the South Africans were very pleased when they got the IDSO report.

'We didn't actually use Karl again, and I'm afraid the poor chap didn't make much money out of his stint. He hadn't bought very well, and when the diamonds were released by the Customs and legally imported by the Diamond Syndicate, they identified the whole parcel as typical Belgian Congo boart – low grade industrial stuff – and valued it at just about the money Karl had spent on it. Karl was very put out by this, and I tipped him £10 for his trouble and bid him goodbye.

'Karl's lists of names and channels resulted in my flying up to Elizabethville and to Dr. Williamson's mine in Tanganyika to see what we could do to block the traffic at its origin. Both mines admitted that they were only too aware of the traffic, and that a steady stream of local prosecutions were taking all the time of their security staffs. Some of this traffic seemed to be following the Nairobi–Salisbury–Lourenço

Marques—Durban air route of East African Airways, and while I was in Rhodesia I decided to do something about blocking this channel.

'It happened that an ex-BOAC steward, whom I will call Patrick Sullivan, was flying on this route. He'd been interviewed by IDSO in London after he'd given evidence for the Crown in the prosecution of other BOAC aircrew for smuggling, and when he came to Africa he contacted me and agreed to work for us.

'Nairobi was the headquarters of East African Airways, and it was also the supply and transport centre for the Williamson Mine, and Sullivan became a regular customer at one of the transit hotels, where he believed one of the waiters was acting as a post-box for the IDB ring working out of Williamson's. Although Sullivan had been mixed up in the London case and so was to a certain extent compromised in the eyes of the local IDB he seemed to the waiter to be a possible carrier, and on my instructions Sullivan agreed to take on the job, for which the smugglers would pay him a fat commission.

'Again I was faced with the danger of turning a man into a licensed smuggler. Although he promised to wire me whenever he was carrying diamonds down to Durban, there was always the possibility that he'd conveniently forget to do so from time to time, and on these occasions would be protected by his work for IDSO. To cover myself, I warned Sullivan that whether he tipped us off that he was carrying stones or not, he would be liable to the usual Customs search, and Sullivan accepted the position.

'Then something very odd happened. I don't say that the IDB had got on to Sullivan's double role, but Sullivan's fate was certainly a curious coincidence. One day I got a cryptic cable from Sullivan asking me to meet him in Durban "to discuss new developments". What these developments were, I never learned, but I guess they were something pretty big.

'Anyway, on the round trip just before the date of our meeting, the East African Airways Dakota in which Sullivan was the steward crashed into the top of Mount Kilimanjaro, the highest mountain in Africa, and all the passengers and crew were killed.'

Blaize shook his head doubtfully, 'I suppose it was just bad luck, but it was certainly good news for the IDB ring operating out of Tanganyika and the Belgian Congo.'

5

ENTER MR. ORFORD

THE LEVANTER WENT ON BLOWING, AND BLAIZE AND I spent a whole day in my room at the Minzah, reading through what I had written and correcting it. I still hadn't got a picture of a straightforward smuggling operation out of a diamond mine, and I asked Blaize a lot of questions about mine security and the various ways of dodging it.

It seemed to me that stealing diamonds from the mine face or the Sort House was no different from any other form of robbery, and in other circumstances the robber takes his booty to a fence who buys his goods and passes them on at a profit. I couldn't get a similar picture of the IDB machinery. Where did the smugglers find a market for their stones? From what Blaize had told me Kimberley and Johannesburg were riddled with police spies and informers, and it seemed to me that a smuggler had very little chance of getting rid of his stones without being caught.

From the notes I made that morning the whole process became a little clearer, particularly because of the entry on the stage of Mr. Henry Orford (that is not his real name), who I expect – though Blaize had no evidence of this – is not the only man in this business.

'Obviously,' said Blaize, 'the first place to stop smuggling is at the mines themselves. At most of the mines this should be easy – at the Kimberley mines, for instance, but in places like Sierra Leone, where the whole country is littered with diamonds, mine security is almost impossible.'

'Supposing I was a European worker. What exactly would happen to me when I went on leave from a place like Consolidated Diamond Mines?'

'You'd be taken by the company bus to the X-ray department and shown into a fine waiting-room with plenty of magazines to read. Your luggage would be put on a conveyor belt that would carry it very slowly into a dark room and under an X-ray scanner with a man sitting above it at some levers to control the speed of the conveyor and stop it.

'He'd be looking down straight through your suitcase. He'd see the scissors and the zip-fasteners and the cufflinks, and all the other metal things in your bag. He'd recognize every black shape at once.

'If there was one he didn't recognize, you'd be asked what it was – perhaps asked to show it or open it. All very polite, like a very refined Customs examination. Then you'd be called through into another room – men into one and women into another – and you'd be X-rayed yourself, with

particular attention to your head and your stomach and your
feet. If the radiographer saw a black speck, in your stomach
for instance, he might tell the mine manager and then you'd
be put in hospital and very politely but thoroughly purged.
On the other hand, the scanner might just make a mark on
a diagram of the human body – everybody has one with his
file – and wait till you went on leave again. If the speck had
altered place, or if there were more specks when he looked
through you again, his suspicions would have been confirmed
and you'd certainly go to the hospital. All very civilized and
polite, as I said. But very thorough. The blacks are treated
in much the same way, but without the waiting-room and
magazines. Often their stomachs are full of black specks.
But these generally turn out to be buttons or nails or pebbles
they've swallowed just to see if the white man's magic really
works or not. Astonishing what they manage to get down
without hurting themselves.'

'In the average mine are there any ways of getting stones
out except through the main gate?'

'It's not easy. Some of these places are like huge concen-
tration camps. Ten feet high electrified double wire fence all
round, and dogs and guards patrolling between the fences day
and night – the De Beers Alsatians are the stars at the local
agricultural shows, by the way. And outside the wire there
are miles of flat, empty ground. No good tunnelling. They've
tried shooting stones out with catapults, but they're nearly
always caught looking for them. And it would have to be
a pretty big stone that wouldn't just disappear in the sand.
They've tried making lead containers to look like household

objects in their luggage. Someone told them – some interested person – that X-rays can't pierce lead. But they're not very good at refined tricks like that. They're mostly content to save their pay and put aside £20 or £30 in their nine months in the compound and then go back up-country to their tribes and blow it. Native mine boys only get about £2 a week upward and their keep. Wages for the management and the trusted men in the Sort House are pretty good, and these people aren't X-rayed when they leave each night. They're trusted. It seems to work. Says a lot for the type of men De Beers employ. Apart from all that, there are one or two really weak spots before the diamonds get from the mine-face to London – opportunities for some determined men to make a million-pound coup, but we won't talk about them. I've told De Beers about them, and I hope they've been coped with by now.

'The great problem when you've stolen a stone and got it through the security check is what to do with it. It's not such a worry for the Europeans. They probably hide their stones away until the right man comes along and they're absolutely certain that he's not a police informer. Or else gradually accumulate a pile and one day resign and go off to Antwerp and walk up and down Pelikaanstraat until they've decided which of the street brokers they like the look of. After that, they'll be quite all right. They'll soon find the right man on Pelikaanstraat, and then they'll have their £50,000 or £100,000 to start a new life with.

'But the black man only wants to get his £10 or £50 and get rid of his stone as quickly as possible. That's where Mr. Henry Orford comes into the picture.

'Mr. Orford is an American and America is the biggest market in the world for diamonds: wherever they come from. For instance, New York is one of the really big terminals for smuggled gem stones as opposed to industrial diamonds. From time to time the US Customs and police make spectacular hauls. One of the biggest cases since the war was in January 1951 when Federal Agents arrested a man called Leiser Weitman at Idlewild. They found £100,000 worth of diamonds in the trick heels of his shoes and later a further £125,000 worth on his body. Weitman got twenty-two months' imprisonment. The Customs men said they stopped him "because he looked nervous". Generally they get a tip-off from some rival smuggling gang. It's a tricky industry.

'Anyway Mr. Henry Orford's operation had nothing to do with smuggling. His line of country was strictly legal.

'In December 1954 one of our contacts received a circular letter. Here it is:'

PO Box – ,
Grand Central Station, New York 17

STRICTLY CONFIDENTIAL – VERY URGENT

Dear Sir,

IMPORT AND EXPORT OF ROUGH DIAMONDS

We have set up a factory in one of the free markets of Europe where we can receive merchandise without any questions or complications. . . . We are ready to pay a good price because only in this way will we have the assurance that you will supply us steadily. . . . This proposition you must keep strictly confidential. . . . We are sure that if you will co-operate with us you will be one of the most successful business men in your country.

Yours very truly,
HENRY ORFORD

'I thought it would be worth while establishing contact with Mr. Orford. He sounded an interesting man. So "Mr. J. Staples" came to life, and wrote to PO Box –, Grand Central Station, and asked how his merchandise should be shipped and in what way payment would be made.

'Mr. Orford's reply – in February '55 – was illuminating. This time he wrote from Frankfurt:'

Postfach –, Frankfurt

Dear Sir,
You must send your merchandise in envelopes of 20 carats each by airmail not registered, merchandise to be glued to the inside wrapper. For your safety, send only your number as your number indicates the sender, and we are the only ones who know by whom shipment was made. Payment will be made in South African pounds by return airmail. Our suggestion to send the diamonds by regular airmail not registered is that this method is safer and quicker, and no one will think for a moment that the package contains rough diamonds. I am very much interested in rough diamonds clean and white in size 2 to 10 pieces per one carat, for which I can

pay 12 to 30 dollars per carat. This opportunity is the greatest in your life.

Yours very truly,

H. ORFORD

'He was also kind enough to enclose this circular exhortation to possible customers:'

STRICTLY CONFIDENTIAL

We are interested to have an agent in whom we can have complete confidence and who will be loyal and trustworthy, because the business we propose to do with you can only be done by a loyal son of Africa who has Africa and Africans uppermost in his heart. Therefore you have been given this greatest of opportunities in your life to make for yourself an undreamed-of fortune amounting to perhaps $1,000,000 yearly (one $ million).

Now, speaking openly, here is what you must be able to do. We are interested that Africans should benefit from the wealth of Africa. Since we are one of the largest and most powerful firms dealing in rough diamonds we would like for you to supply us with rough diamonds and thereby enrich yourself and other Africans. We would like to point out to you that the rough diamonds belong to your people because it comes from their lands and grounds, even though others may claim it.

Don't forget that since these rough diamonds belong to you and your people you can do with it whatever you like, and according to the customs of the free democratic world anyone who does not allow the free trade of African merchandise by Africans is certainly the ILLEGAL party.

If you feel confident that you are able to make the proper contacts and also to carry through successfully the organization of this business, we will then instruct you how to run this business with us without any risk to yourself whatsoever.

This letter is strictly confidential and upon your honour as an African it must not be allowed to fall into the wrong hands.

Awaiting your reply immediately, we remain as always, your friend in confidence.

'You see his ingenious line. He was appealing to the black African heart of Mr. J. Staples. And Mr. J. Staples fell for his line and wrote to Frankfurt to say that he had a small packet of 34 stones weighing 10 carats for sale for £20.

'Orford took the bait, allotted Staples a code number – 3 J. S. – and sent him these shipping instructions:'

STRICTLY CONFIDENTIAL

SUPPLIER NO. 3 J. S.

SHIPPING CONDITIONS FOR

ROUGH DIAMONDS

This is to advise you how to ship merchandise to us so as to cut your own shipping expenses to a minimum, and for this reason to receive the highest possible price in the whole wide world.

If you ship according to our instructions you will receive 30 per cent more than anyone else will pay you, because in this way we can save and, in turn, pay you the extra saving in cost, thus enhancing your profits.

1. You will send merchandise to us in plain airmail envelopes (NOT REGISTERED). If not registered it will be delivered immediately without delay, for the reason that the Customs Regulations in the United States provide that if the shipment is not valued over $250 it does not need any entry permit, and rough diamonds are completely duty free in the USA.

In this way we will receive the merchandise in New York without any trouble and in accordance with the USA Customs Regulations, within four days from any part of the world.

You can send merchandise in a very simple manner, just using sealing tape (Scotch tape or adhesive tape) and fasten the stones to a piece of paper and insert them in the envelope where the Post Office will not stamp over them.

In sending merchandise to us, use ONLY your Supply Number, which gives you the security that no one – irrespective of where located – will know who the supplier is. The envelopes in which you send merchandise should not contain letters, only merchandise and invoice, which must state the number of carats or how many pieces are contained in the envelope. And the invoice must not show over $250 worth of merchandise. You may rest assured that we will pay you the highest possible price, no matter what the amount is stated on the invoice.

THE CONTENTS OF EACH ENVELOPE MUST NOT BE
MORE THAN 20 CARATS.

PAYMENT. On the same day that we receive merchandise from you, we will make payment to you in any of the following ways:

Cash in letters in any currency you desire;

Cheques to any branch of any bank in the whole world, not disclosing the name of the sender;

Cable drafts to any bank, to any address in any name you wish.

If you follow our instructions to the letter, which is essential, you can be very successful, because these instructions have been proven successful by past experience without any risks to you, the sender. For this reason we are always able to pay the highest possible price immediately upon receipt of merchandise.

'Henry Orford also enclosed a declaration form, of which this is a Photostat after Staples had filled in the details, including the photographs of the actual stones he sent.

'Meanwhile, we informed our IDSO agent in Germany, who checked up with the German Customs authorities. In due course they pounced on Henry Orford's incoming mail, including the packet from 3 J.S. As a result of this and other action in Germany, they got hold of a list of most of Orford's illicit suppliers in Africa, and quite a number of "brother Africans" found themselves in jail.

'There was a pause on the Orford front, and then he was back with this letter:'

Dear Mr. Staples,

I wish to inform you that my husband now is coming along very well after being badly wounded in an air crash. For this reason you have not received any orders from him.

My best regards,
Yours very truly,
MRS. ORFORD

'J. Staples came into action with a shipment of five carats in a plain envelope direct to the old German address.

'But by this time Henry Orford's intelligence machine – which must have been a good one – had caught up with J. Staples, and we received this sharp rap over the knuckles:'

June 11th, 1956
Dear Mr. Staples,

Our general policy with our suppliers is to be truthful. You have sent us 5 carats of merchandise which were seized by the German authorities. We can get this back very easily, but the fine would cost us more than we can win. In any event, we will have this merchandise free.

Your case is a different one. We have information that you are co-operating completely with the English authorities, both in England and South Africa. For this reason we are not sending you 20 South African pounds, as you requested.

For us, if we can trust a supplier in South Africa, it is not a question of his making half a million pounds a year without any risk. Give us proof of your loyalty to us that you really mean to do business with us and we will change our opinion about you, and we will give you the greatest opportunity, such as comes once in a lifetime.

We are awaiting your reply,
Yours very truly,
H. ORFORD

'Mr. J. Staples was thoroughly "blown" so we regretfully handed the whole case over to the American Customs. One of these days I shall be interested to hear what finally happened to the ingenious Mr. Orford.'

6

THE MILLION-POUND GAMBLE

BLAIZE WAS LATE FOR HIS RENDEZVOUS IN THE GARDEN of the Minzah. When he turned up, he said he had spent most of the night in a night-club. There he had found himself buying interminable Cuba libres, which is rum and Coca-Cola, for one of the girls in the cabaret. He was pretty sure there had been no rum in the Coca-Cola and that the drink was just a substitute for the traditional 'whiskies and water' which are really weak tea. The girl had been attractive, but Blaize had disgraced himself by falling asleep during the cabaret and missing her act (Blaize said he always fell asleep during cabarets in night-clubs). The evening hadn't been a success, and Blaize had finally got back to his hotel at five in the morning after the girl, much to his relief, had parted with the also traditional 'Pas ce soir. Peut-etre demain.'

This was my cue to ask Blaize if he had come across

many women in the smuggling racket – beautiful couriers, glamorous shills in the mining towns, and so on. Blaize said sadly that the only beautiful girls he had come across had been on the side of the angels. They were the girls in the Sorting-Room on the top floor of the Diamond Corporation's headquarters in Johannesburg. One day he was leaving the building when the girls were clocking out. It was pouring with rain and Blaize had given one of the girls a lift home. She knew that Blaize had something to do with security (he was the subject of much gossip in the Diamond Corporation), and she admitted that boy-friends sometimes jokingly propositioned her to get them some diamonds. One of the ways they'd suggested was that she should grow her fingernails long and pack them with wax.

Every day she'd be able to pick up a few tiny stones. The small loss of weight from her day's production wouldn't be noticed, but the stolen carats would mount up fast. The girl told Blaize that she didn't think anyone had fallen for this sort of trick. The girls were well paid and took a lot of pride in their work.

In general, Blaize said that diamond smugglers didn't trust women. They had found that the stones were too much of a temptation. Only one woman, and an entirely innocent one at that, had crossed the path of IDSO and she had been incidental to IDSO's biggest coup – a coup so big they had had to call in the Government to finance it. Blaize said: 'Up to now I've tried to give you some idea of what I and the rest of the IDSO team had been doing in South Africa and in the East, and I've put off talking about West Africa,

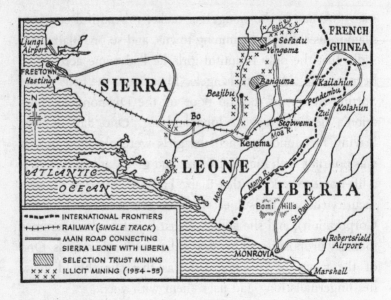

and particularly Sierra Leone, where there's been the biggest smuggling operation in the world.

'The position there is that Sierra Leone Selection Trust used to own the mining and prospecting rights over the whole country. But Sierra Leone is more or less solid bush and jungle, and in fact Selection Trust had been concentrating on about 130 square miles round a place called Yengema. This was supposed to be a Diamond Protection Area, where nobody can live or work without a licence from the District Commissioner, but in practice you can't fence and patrol 130 square miles of bush, and the place was more or less wide open to illicit diggers. The position was farcical. For instance, when I found my way round the area, I saw a fine new saloon parked outside a broken down store in one of the villages. I asked John Gundry – he was the mine manager at Yengema at the time and a splendid chap – who it belonged to. He said: "Well, I got one of those not long ago, and the local IDB regarded it as a matter of pride to keep at least on a par with the mine manager."

'You see, for years the Government hadn't enough money or police to do anything about it. Gundry had got his security staff, but Bernard Nealon, who is head of the CID in Freetown, had only one assistant, and although the Sierra Leone police force, under an excellent Commissioner – Bill Syer – are a fine lot of men, there was a general idea among the illicit miners that the soil of Sierra Leone belongs to the Sierra Leoneans.

'And Sierra Leone is littered with diamonds, mostly along the courses of the rivers – the Bafi and Sewa, for instance, and smaller streams like the Woa, Tavi and Moa – hundreds of miles of streams and swamp. Even with thousands of police and helicopters and God knows what, you couldn't do much about illegal mining over that sort of area. The gangs of pot-holers came along every night and got to work along the banks of these rivers. They slept during the daytime. If you flew round in a small aircraft or hacked your way through the bush, you could see the banks freshly pock-marked with diggings every morning.

'I had a bad attack of fever in October '54 and then went up to Freetown to look into the shambles. It was called Freetown at the end of the eighteenth century when we populated the Colony with 400 freed Negro slaves and sixty white prostitutes from the English ports. Extraordinary story. Other tribes from French Guinea and Liberia and God knows where else seeped into the country at various times, and now there's a fantastic mixture of natives plus a handful of English officials and business men. There are practically no other European visitors except an occasional commercial traveller putting up in the one hotel – the City Hotel – which has twelve bedrooms. It's not much of a town. One's almost ashamed of its being an English possession – particularly after visiting Leopoldville or Elizabethville in the Belgian Congo, which are as spick and span as Brussels or Antwerp. Of course, the Belgians haven't got a big colonial empire, and they can afford to spend plenty of money and energy on what they have got. We've got bits and pieces of territory all round the world, and not enough money and enthusiasm to go round. At any rate, there's no doubt that Sierra Leone comes pretty near the bottom of the pile.

'Luckily, I was put up at the Selection Trust rest-house at Hill Station, above Freetown, where Government officials have their bungalows. It's the Ritz compared with the stews of Freetown. But it's on the edge of the jungle – as I was reminded by finding a king cobra on the veranda one morning. The servants killed it. I sat up there for several days talking things over with Nealon of the CID, and then went up through the jungle to Yengema to hear the Selection Trust side of the story. They're wonderful men, working away for their company in this godforsaken place, but from the point of view of security the position was hopeless. The screening plants are miles apart and very isolated. If the local security officer wanted to contact one of these plants or the police he had to send a jeep through the bush and across a river practically paved with crocodiles by a ferry which operated only by day, and not at all when the river was in spate. There wasn't even a walkie-talkie system. When I was there the Security Chief, Harry Morgan, got a message from an informer that digging was going on a few miles away from Yengema. He got some of his men together and sent a call for a few African police to help make arrests. By the time they'd found their way to the scene of the digging, the miners had vanished into the night, leaving more than two hundred pits behind them. The canisters full of diamonds from Yengema reach the airport at Freetown twice a month after an incredible trek in a train that averages eleven mph over a single track that's always washing away. Just before I arrived two fat consignments had disappeared somewhere between Freetown and England, and one loss hadn't been noticed until days later.

'So you see the picture – utter confusion, and the country wide open to illicit mining.'

I asked: 'Where does the smuggling come in? How do the miners get their stones out of the country, and where to?'

Blaize said: 'There's 200 miles of open frontier with Liberia, and a continuous stream of Mandingo natives crossing over. They're a very bright tribe, and buy the stones from the diggers for a pittance and take them over the first stage of the smuggling route to Monrovia, the capital of Liberia. There they sell them to the hordes of Antwerp and other dealers. Monrovia's crawling with these types from Belgium and Beirut. These dealers put up the Mandingoes in hotels and pay all their expenses and carry them round in taxis and lush them up with wrist-watches and fat cigars and buy their diamonds quite openly and – for that matter – quite legally. The Liberians turn a blind eye to the whole traffic. The sale of export licences and dealers' permits brings a fortune into the country and into the pockets of Negro officials, and there's a perfectly respectable whitewash. You see, the myth is that these diamonds are Liberian diamonds from the Liberian diamond mines. These mines don't exist, of course. I'll tell you later about the only one that does.'

I said, 'How big was the traffic?'

Blaize shrugged his shoulders. 'Even the Governor of Sierra Leone admitted it was around seven million pounds – far more than the annual production of Sierra Leone Selection Trust. But I put it at nearer ten million. That was only a guess, and based on the buying operations we got started in Monrovia. I'm coming to that. You see, about this time we had a stroke of luck. A German diamond dealer from Monrovia whom I'll call Willy Rosen contacted Nealon and gave him the whole picture, and Nealon passed on the gist of Rosen's story to me. I saw the light, wrote out my report, packed my bags and flew to London. One factor put the wind under my tail. Willy Rosen had told Nealon that he would come over to our side.

'I don't know exactly what Willy Rosen's motives were and I still don't now – partly money, but more important probably, Rosen, who'd been a refugee for most of his life, wanted to get away from Liberia and settle in the West. He wanted a passport into British business and – for both he and his wife had social ambitions – into British society.

'Willy Rosen was born in Stuttgart. His parents were

German Jews. His father died when he was thirteen and he went to school for three years in Switzerland. By the time he was seventeen Hitler had started his pogroms, and Rosen fled to South Africa, where he tried various jobs. After the war he met Lisl, his future wife, who was working in Johannesburg. Lisl is the woman I was telling you about, but she has only a walk-on part in the story. After various vicissitudes, they set up an agency business in Liberia, and Willy's energy and charm, combined with Lisl's intelligence, made them stand out in the sleazy community. Rosen got hold of some good import agencies, and by 1954, when we met up with him, he had six German clerks working for him. And he'd gone into the diamond business. He'd also invested in local property. This showed that, unlike other European traders, he had a genuine stake in the country. And Rosen's meticulous adherence to import and export regulations and his reputation for expecting only a small profit on his turnover had made a favourable impression in Liberian Government circles from which he and, incidentally, we were later to profit.

'When this was reported to Sillitoe in London, it was agreed that we should use Rosen and finance his activities. We passed this information back to Freetown CID. Any doubts we might have had about Rosen's effectiveness were quickly dispelled. Rosen flew up to Freetown on November 25th, made a secret rendezvous with Nealon, and disclosed that a Lebanese diamond dealer, one of whose many names was Finkle, had invited Rosen to inspect a packet of illegal diamonds with a view to running them into Liberia.

'Rosen was due to see Finkle on the night of Sunday the

28th and he suggested that Nealon should raid the meeting. Nealon agreed, and on that night, in the stinking heat, he had his men round the house. Unfortunately, as it turned out, he wasn't able to block all possible escape routes for fear of attracting attention.

'After giving Rosen twenty minutes to get into the negotiations, Nealon and three of his men who had been waiting in the garden smashed down the door and burst into the living-room. Pandemonium broke out, and there was a free-for-all fight. Finkle, a smart fighter with quick reactions, kicked Rosen in the face and, helped by three other Lebanese, dived through the window. He crashed twenty-five feet on to a watering-can in the next-door garden, but nothing was broken and he disappeared into the night. His wife, Dolores, who was heavy with child, showed signs of giving premature birth, but was calmed by Nealon and his men. When order had been restored, thirty five diamonds were picked up from the floor and next day Finkle was traced and arrested on a charge of illegal possession. The charge was never heard. Somehow Finkle fled the country. He was blacklisted as a prohibited immigrant, and many months later we traced him to the house of a well-known diamond merchant in Beirut.

'Anyway, Rosen's behaviour had proved his loyalty and in January 1955 we flew him to London to talk business – and it was interesting business. In London Rosen revealed that over the previous three months his exports of diamonds from Monrovia had progressively risen until his last parcel in December had been worth nearly $100,000. Rosen assured us that he could maintain his purchases at least at the December level and after a certain amount of palaver it was agreed in London that we should use Rosen as our secret buyer in Monrovia. We would try to buy up the entire Liberian leak and funnel the smuggled diamonds out of the black channels into the legal sales organization in London.

'There was one big snag. Rosen had to pay out dollars in Liberia for his diamonds and he would have to be supplied with dollars to purchase for the Diamond Corporation. But dollars to the amount we needed were hard to come by and the only solution was to take the whole story to the British Government and put our cards on the table. Thanks to the importance of the diamond trade to Britain, Whitehall needed very little persuading. They were particularly influenced by the fact that industrial stones being sold in Monrovia were being bought up by an agent for Russia and were going via Antwerp and Zurich through the Iron Curtain to be used in the Russian armaments industry. They were also impressed by the fact that we would be taking off the black market huge consignments of diamonds which ought to be earning dollars through legitimate British trade with America.

'To cut a long story short, the powers that be agreed to back us with an initial half a million pounds in dollars, and later, when we'd spent this huge sum, they put up another half-million.'

Blaize chuckled. 'Not bad, getting Her Majesty's Government to have a million-pound fling! These Civil Servants have plenty of guts. There was practically no arguing, and the gigantic scheme was put through in a matter of hours.'

7

SENATOR WITHERSPOON'S
DIAMOND MINE

From the first, Tangier had been passionately intrigued by our presence in the town. It is a small place, and a new English face is a novelty. Blaize and I and the admirable Miss Dorothy Cooper, who had been in the Foreign Service and who typed my manuscript, went through a daily inquisition. My own presence was explicable. I was probably writing a thriller based on Tangier or perhaps articles on Morocco for my paper, but who was Blaize? It was quickly discovered – by an inquiry at the airline offices perhaps – that he had flown up from Zululand, and it was clear from his conversation that he knew his Africa. But what did he *do*? Blaize was non-committal: 'Sort of research work,' he would say vaguely, and change the subject. I did not get off so lightly. I had several good friends in Tangier and they were determined to penetrate the secret of me and my 'Zulu'.

With my back to the wall I hinted that I was writing a book on a scientific subject. Had they ever heard of the coelacanth? It could be that Blaize was an expert on this famous 'missing link' fish.

How boring! My friends, their eyes glazing with indifference, dropped the subject. No one in Dean's Bar – *the* bar of Tangier – cared about coelacanths, and no one knew enough about them to ask questions. It soon got about that Blaize was the man who had discovered the coelacanth. He had caught one alive. It was in his bath at the hotel.

Blaize was delighted with his 'cover'. He suggested we should have built a curious-shaped oblong container which he would carry about. Occasionally he would lift the lid and peer in, and perhaps drop in scraps of exotic food. We agreed that this would be going too far. Blaize didn't often laugh; but he laughed about the coelacanth and he also laughed when he told me the story of Senator Witherspoon's diamond mine. He told me the story in a café in the Socco Chico, which is the 'thieves' kitchen' of Tangier. It is here that crooks and smugglers and dope-pedlars congregate, and a pretty villainous gang they are. Blaize said: 'The Rosen operation went along smoothly, and by the end of June we'd spent most of our million-pound fund and succeeded in upsetting the whole underground diamond trading fraternity of Monrovia. Several dealers found the crumbs of business left over from Rosen's feast inadequate to pay their overheads, and they packed up and left. We'd also got a pretty good estimate of the total leakage through Liberia, and we agreed that the amount of smuggling from Sierra Leone Selection Trust concessions was at least three times the total production of the mines. 'Rosen had done well for us, but also for himself, as he was paid a bonus of £15,000 for running the operation and Lisl Rosen was presented with a diamond ring fit for a duchess. On the other hand it gradually leaked out that Rosen was operating for us, and his position in Monrovia became not only invidious but even precarious, and he received constant threats of violence from gangsters hired by his rivals.

'But he was a tough, cheerful little man, and the last time I heard of him he was doing well at his old stand.

'While our million-pound buying operation was going on, IDSO was working on this myth of the Liberian diamond mines which the Liberians obstinately maintained were the source of the diamonds flooding out of the country. We found out the answer to that riddle, and I'd like to know when the British Government is going to take the whole thing up with Liberia. You see, once a packet of diamonds gets a legal export licence from any country in the world, it's perfectly legal merchandise, and the flood of "Liberian" diamonds pouring into Antwerp, for instance, is a perfectly legal flood, which the Belgian Government can't do anything about. The stones are legally imported into Belgium and go to the brokers on Pelikaanstraat, and from there a lot of them are then re-exported to respectable cover addresses in Zurich and out of Switzerland again behind the Iron Curtain.

'So we wanted to know for certain if there really were any diamond mines in Liberia. On the face of it, there was no reason why there shouldn't be, and our geologists said it was quite possible that Liberian rivers were carrying diamonds along their courses as is the case in Sierra Leone. We had nothing to go on, and the British and American Embassies in Monrovia, who were equally worried about the problem, had also drawn a complete blank. The Liberian Government refused to disclose any information about the location of the mines or their production figures. Fortunately, in March 1955, Senator the Honourable William N. Witherspoon came on the scene, and Senator Witherspoon happened to be chairman of the Liberian House of Representatives Committee of Mines and Mining.

'Senator Witherspoon wrote to the managing director of Selection Trust in London to say that he was the owner of certain diamond mining rights in Liberia and that he needed help and capital to exploit them, and he offered to call on Selection Trust in London to talk the position over.

'IDSO advised Selection Trust to appear interested, and in due course the Negro Senator arrived in London and at his first meeting with Selection Trust admitted the only diamond workings were on his own concession – the Dubred Company at Zui, in the jungle about a hundred miles north of Monrovia.

'The Senator said he had already cleared an area of jungle for use as an airstrip. He now wanted Sierra Leone Selection Trust to put up the capital and provide the machinery to work his concession. If they agreed, he would offer them a two-thirds share in the project.

'This seemed a wonderful opportunity to penetrate the whole Liberian diamond myth, and we advised Selection

Trust to say that they would give the Senator an answer when two of their geologists had examined the site.

'Senator Witherspoon agreed, and Selection Trust chose Mr. P. M. R. Willis, their senior field geologist, and Harry Morgan, the Chief Security Officer at Yengema, who was quite capable of passing as a prospector.

'At the beginning of April Senator Witherspoon wrote that he was ready for Morgan and Willis, but his letter suggested that he was interested as much in diamond dealing as in diamond mining.'

Blaize shuffled among his papers. 'Here's what he says on April 7th, 1955, writing from 19 Clay Street, Monrovia:'

At long last our mining difficulties have been overcome and I attach hereto copies of the Acts of the Legislature of Liberia recently passed and published in handbills relating to said subject. This gives you information how things are done now in relation to mining in this Republic.

I received a letter from the Manager of your Company in Sierra Leone informing me that Messrs. Morgan and Willis are the elected persons to visit me in Liberia and a request for their visas. I have made this request to our State Department today and I shall inform them instantly I receive the instruction from our Department of State.

I may here say that diamond purchasing in Liberia is a very lucrative business these days now that the law is passed. The quantity that can be purchased daily may exceed any capital invested. The Act to Amend Customs Tariff, etc., points the way how same can be carried on. We (you and I) can therefore form a Liberian partnership instantly, evince certificate from any bank in the world that we are worth ten thousand dollars ($10,000.00) and then start and get rich overnight. Of course, although the law permits me to a fifty percentum right in the said partnership, and although the agreement will say so, yet I shall never require this. I am sure we can do good business. There are many diamond purchasers here but many times lack capital which causes their customers to lose confidence in them and their financial ability. If an investment comes to Liberia with capital, conforms to Liberian law, with proper direction, which I am ready to give, their purchase will be illimitable.

I shall be glad therefore if you can look into this matter seriously and if possible instruct your men to open with me negotiation in the matter and in fact set up our company and even whilst they are here, they can make wonderful purchases only provide them with the capital to buy with. When it comes to capital, we do not need too much as we could make weekly shipments and our investment could be recurring decimal.

Out here, I am prepared to board and lodge your men in my house and home, give them all legal direction and safeguards, and bring them the goods to buy. What more?

Please cable me immediately using Bentley Edition

5th whether your men should live with me in my house or in a hotel and your reaction to my proposition about buying diamonds.

If you agree with me to buy diamonds, your profits from this source alone can carry our mining efforts which I am sure will be most successful for I shall show your men samples and proofs when they get here. Besides, the entire Liberia is open to me and I can secure prospecting licences in keeping with our laws for any part thereof by complying with the laws. All I need from you is know-how and capital.

Please answer this most urgent letter immediately. I am much better now.

Yours very truly,
WILLIAM N. WITHERSPOON

'Selection Trust were not dismayed. In order to get the vital intelligence needed on Liberia they agreed that we should go ahead with the original plan, but should naturally stall any proposals for setting up a buying business. It was also decided that we should tell Morgan and Willis nothing about Rosen's operation. We were glad of the opportunity to get an independent picture of the Monrovian diamond trade. They took off from Freetown on May 10th, and did a really splendid job. Here's Morgan's diary which came with their report to IDSO, and I can't do better than give it you as it stands.'

Morgan's Diary

May, 10th

Willis and I flew into Monrovia and were met by Mr. Witherspoon and escorted to Johnson's Hotel, Broad Street. Travelling in the plane with us was Henry Brasseur, a dealer who was returning from Europe. We passed through the Immigration Department, were photographed, had our fingerprints taken and signed a form stating we were not Communists. My profession on this form was stated to be 'mine operator'.

May, 11th

Met Witherspoon in the morning to formulate our plans. We made it quite clear to him that they must include a visit to all or any diamond mines in Liberia. He informed us quite definitely that there was only one diamond mine in Liberia, 'his', or that of the Dubred Company at Zui, approximately one hundred miles north-north-west of Monrovia which could be reached only by air or on foot.

Witherspoon suggested that there were probably other diamond deposits but was emphatic that no others were being mined and said he would know, being Chairman of the Committee of Mines and Mining.

That there was no other diamond mining taking place in Liberia we confirmed through personal observation and by asking many independent people. There was never a suggestion from any of these people that there was any diamond mine in Liberia other than that at Zui.

At this meeting, Witherspoon suggested our Company might like to open a diamond-buying agency in Liberia. As instructed by London Office my reply was to the effect that London was awaiting with interest a parcel of diamonds he had promised, so that they could study the type of diamonds available for sale. His suggestion that we open a buying agency gave me an excuse for asking pertinent questions about quantities available for purchase, what competition we would have and from whom, also his reason for wanting us to open the agency (answer – 5 or 10 per cent commission). I also used the question of the agency as an excuse for asking to see some diamonds in Monrovia.

May, 12th
In the evening we were taken to visit 'Willy Rosen', German diamond buyer who employs two diamond experts thirty years in the business.

Rosen showed us several packets of diamonds, 99 per cent being of the Sierra Leone type which I estimated to weigh not less than 3000 or 4000 carats which he said was the result of two days' buying from Sierra Leone Mandingoes.

From one parcel he produced a few stones which he described as typical Liberian diamonds; five or six to a carat, rounded stones, similar to those produced in French Guinea but with a higher proportion of serie (gem).

Rosen said quite openly that his diamonds came

from Sierra Leone and in embarrassing quantities. This frank statement in no way embarrassed Witherspoon but seemed to please him as it substantiated his claim that there were enough diamonds available to justify our opening a buying agency. From Rosen we went to the Studor Hotel where Brasseur lives, partner with Julius Belcher in the Dubred Mining Company Ltd. We met Brasseur and with him an Armenian, Ardavast Powanlian, normally resident at Zui and in charge of the mining operations there. Brasseur showed us 15 carats of diamonds just brought down by Ardavast, also about 500 carats Sierra Leone type diamonds which he said he had bought in Liberia. He seemed flabbergasted when told we were going to Zui and it was obviously the first he had heard of it although he was a partner in the Company operating there.

From there we went to an ice cream parlour where an Egyptian, Kheir, produced and offered for sale a 64-carat serie diamond. It was by now 12:15 midnight. Two weeks later we saw the same stone in a better light at the house of Willy Rosen who had paid £30 a carat for it.

After seeing all these diamonds, Witherspoon again told us what a good thing it would be if our Company opened a buying agency.

May, 13th to 15th
During this period we bought camp kit, food, and arranged the charter plane to carry us to Zui on the 16th.

We visited the British Consul, David Mitchel, and

the British Ambassador, Mr. Capper. Capper expressed himself astonished at the Liberians allowing us to visit the mines and inspect the diamond production as they had never before allowed any representatives of the British Government or any reputable British firm to do this, even having refused permission for such people to inspect a packet of diamonds seized from smugglers. He asked if possible to be sent a copy of our report through the Foreign Office.

The American Chargé d'Affaires, Frank Wile, offered to give any help possible. He seemed very concerned about East-West trade in diamonds. He has promised to forward me some figures of diamond exports from Liberia.

Brasseur quite early realized the significance of our visit and before we left endeavoured to discourage us from venturing up-country, telling us that the airstrip at Zui was unsafe now that the rains were here and the pilot would not risk landing there unless pressure was brought to bear on him. Further that the diamond mine was six and a half hours' walk through fever-ridden jungle, fraught with hazards from wild animals, mentioning bison (bush cows), elephants and leopards.

May, 16th

Flew to Zui in chartered plane, one-passenger Piper Cub, HB OOX, piloted by Max Pop, self first with all camp equipment packed round me in the cockpit followed three hours later by Willis and an African servant of

Witherspoon's, Robert Johnson, who crouched in the luggage space behind the passenger seat.

The airstrip was found to be adequate and the only wild animals we saw in the interior were monkeys and hippopotami. The walk from the airstrip to the town of Zui was about one mile and from there to the mining camp a further eleven miles, three and a half hours' hard walking, involving one crossing of the River Mano by canoe.

The Dubred Mining Company's camp, the only diamond mine in Liberia, consists of a few native palm-leaf-roofed houses with mud walls (in one of which we lived) capable of accommodating at most between fifty and seventy natives, but occupied at the time of our visit by only twelve people excluding our bearers.

The mine which we visited consisted of a small clearing in the bush half a mile from the camp on the River Kumbor, and has a worked-out surface area of approximately 2500 square yards only (fifty yards square). Nine men were working on the mine during the period of our visit, using primitive equipment and treating approximately one cubic yard a day. Their equipment consisted of three joplin jigs, one set of foot sizing rockers, headpans and shovels.

The headman at the mine, Francis Gballeh, had been instructed to give no help and for the first two or three days was obstructive. He was given a few presents and before we left volunteered much information and showed me diamonds recovered from the working during the period we were there. They conformed to the type of Liberian diamonds shown us in Monrovia and were similar to the one diamond we ourselves recovered from a pot-hole in the bed of the Kumbor stream, 200 yards below the mine.

May, 17th

The Armenian, Ardavast, visited us at the camp. He warned us against working in his mine, saying that he would be forced to prevent us should we try. He wanted us to give a promise that we would send him or Brasseur a copy of our report but we were non-committal. He fortunately didn't stay long, having walked twelve miles to deal with us and having to return the same day.

May, 18th

Dug out pot-holes in Kumbor and washed the gravel in search for concentrate and diamonds. Found one small Liberian-type diamond. There was no possibility of it having been planted, Willis and I doing the work.

Our equipment, furnished by Senator Witherspoon, consisted of four zinc bathtubs, the bottoms of which had been removed and replaced by wire screening, of sizes from eight mm. down to one mm. With these we screened and jigged.

May, 19th

Fruitless twenty-five-mile walk to and from Zui to meet plane chartered to take us on reconnaissance flight. The plane did not arrive until 3:30 when we were two miles along the track on the way back to reach camp before nightfall.

May, 20th to 24th
During this period we did a little pitting and a lot of walking looking for other signs of current mining and gathering information from anyone who would talk. We concluded that there was no other diamond mining in the vicinity of Zui.

It is quite obvious that the mine at Zui is not an economic proposition.

Willis was not able to walk back to Sierra Leone as originally planned, for two reasons. First he developed blood poisoning from leg wounds which incapacitated him for two days, and secondly while we were at Zui a letter was received from Witherspoon warning us against trying to cross the border because of the activities of the Liberian Army and he did not want us to be 'humiliated'.

May, 25th
Returned to Monrovia.

May, 26th
We met [name omitted: I. F.] shortly passing through England. This man asked me for a letter of introduction to London Office as he was carrying a packet of diamonds which he wished to sell. I warned him of the risk involved in carrying diamonds to which he replied:

'Say that I've got a diplomatic passport.'

In the afternoon, visited the Bureau of Mines and Geology and met the Liberian director, Arthur Sherman, and were invited to his home which we visited. He was very interested in our activities, somewhat suspicious and very non-committal.

Supper with Willy Rosen, more gossip.

May, 27th

Visited Immigration Department to get exit visas, not granted as Police Captain had received complaints from the Department of Justice that we had violated rules by visiting the interior. Told Witherspoon who later accompanied us to the Immigration Department, handed our passports to the Police Captain with the order 'Sign these', and we left saying 'Thank you for your cooperation, Captain'.

May, 28th

Diamond buyers of Liberia are reputed to have held a meeting to discuss what action they could take against Willy Rosen who was buying at such high prices and running his business so efficiently that he was getting all the trade. They propose putting the matter in front of President Tubman and complaining that Willy Rosen is an agent for the Diamond Corporation.

May, 29th

Great efforts to get figures of diamonds exported from

Liberia were made. No one could or would produce these, the only published figures being the figure of 20,000 carats for 1954. These could not have come from the Liberian mines. The American Chargé d'Affaires, trying at the same time, was also unsuccessful in obtaining figures.

Drinks at the Embassy that night. We had to leave early to meet President Tubman, but the President did not turn up.

May, 30th

Brasseur and Belcher visited us at Johnson Hotel on May 30th, one and a half hours before we left the country and in rather a truculent mood asked what we had been doing up-country. We referred them to the Honourable Witherspoon and they said Witherspoon had sold all his interests in the mine to them in return for 10 per cent of any profits made and could produce documents to prove it. I answered that our lawyers would, of course, wish to peruse all relevant documents before starting mining operations. At this stage Witherspoon arrived and escorted us to the airfield.

14:00 hours – flew to Freetown.

When I had finished reading Blaize commented sourly: 'So much for Senator Witherspoon's diamond mine and so much, incidentally, for the millions of pounds' worth of "Liberian" diamonds that pour out into the world every year.'

8

THE HEART OF THE MATTER

FOR THE MOST PART, BLAIZE'S COMMENTS ON THE MEN he had met during his three years were kindly. He referred to the smugglers in the amused, fatherly way that policemen often use when they talk of the crooks they have caught. Blaize showed no resentment over the occasional obstructiveness of officials. They were doing their jobs, and he realized how irritating it must have been to have this mysterious man from London, with Sir Ernest Oppenheimer behind him, poking about asking questions and making recommendations which reflected on their efficiency.

But Blaize was scathing about Liberia – with good cause as we have seen. He despised many of the comic opera Negroes in official positions, but he thought even less of the white men who backed them and often incited them in their venality. Liberia was, after all, the first Negro State, and

Utopia in the imagination of coloured peoples all over the world, and if this was to be the pattern of Negro emancipation Blaize didn't hold out much hope for the future of Ghana and the Federation of the West Indies.

Blaize was also critical of certain members of the former Government of Sierra Leone. He hadn't liked the way they had seemed to avert their gaze while the whole of a British colony disintegrated. In the account of the wide-open illicit digging and diamond smuggling in Sierra Leone which follows, I have considerably watered down Blaize's criticisms of the Guilty Men who stood and watched while a whole British colony lost its name.

'You can see,' said Blaize, 'that by halfway through '55 we'd more or less got the whole picture of what amounted collectively to the greatest smuggling operation in the world. There were the small leaks from the Kimberley mines and perhaps occasionally from Consolidated Diamond Mines at Oranjemund. There was a trickle from the Belgian Congo and from Williamson's mine in Tanganyika. These were mostly problems of physical security, and we'd made our various recommendations which generally amounted to reducing the number of men who had a chance of handling the diamonds between the mine-face and the manager's safe. So far as the IDB population was concerned – the smugglers and illegal buyers and cutters – we had seen quite a lot of arrests made and hundreds of names blacklisted, but all this was nothing compared with the flood from Sierra Leone which was not so much organized smuggling as a complete collapse of law and authority throughout the whole of a

British colony nearly as big as Ireland. It was certainly not Sierra Leone Selection Trust's fault. The diamond industry in Sierra Leone might never have been heard of but for Selection Trust's pioneering. It was the fault of drift, of weak local government and of ignorance in Whitehall. At the time we came on the scene in 1954, nobody, even in Selection Trust or the Sierra Leone Government, appreciated the extent to which illegal mining in the interior was getting out of control; but within a matter of months the situation had so deteriorated that anyone reading the local papers would have thought it was Sierra Leone Selection Trust rather than the illegal diggers who were breaking the laws and ruining the country. All this ended with a partial collapse of administration and with the serious rioting which broke out over most of Sierra Leone at the end of 1955, which led to the Commission of Inquiry under Sir Herbert Cox. You can read all about it in the Cox White Paper, but this passage – ' Blaize was leafing through the White Paper, and he now ran his pencil down one long paragraph – 'will give you the picture. This is what the Commission says:'

We have found, and, therefore we have described, a degree of demoralization among the people in their customary institutions and in their approach to the statutory duties with which they have been entrusted, which has shocked us. Dishonesty has become accepted as a normal ingredient of life to such an extent that no one has been concerned to fight it or even complain about it. The ordinary peasant or fisherman seems originally to have accepted a degree of corruption which was tolerable; at a later stage he has been cowed into accepting it; finally he rebelled . . . there has developed such a lack of confidence in others, such a mistrust of authority that the restoration of self-respect and of some belief even in the possibility of integrity will be hard to achieve.

'Anyway, all that's politics, and I'm only trying to show you that there was no point in doing any intelligence or security work in that sort of atmosphere. We did what we could to help the police and we formed up again and again to the Government to try and get something done. But the officials we saw did little but nod sagely and maintain an attitude of enigmatic neutrality – even when there was a general strike and rioting in Freetown and at Yengema in February '55 and several hundred of the rioters tried to smash up the mine. It was only thanks to the guts of John Gundry, the mine manager, and people like Harry Morgan, that the European families at the mine weren't all hacked to death. Guns and tear gas kept the hordes at bay, and in due course they disappeared into the bush and returned to their illicit pot-holing for which all these disturbances had provided excellent cover.

'At about that time the Commissioner of Income Tax decided to require all IDB suspects to disclose what remittances they had received from overseas during the previous three years, and what they'd done with the money. He had reason to believe that the local banks had received more than three million pounds from abroad during the past twelve months alone, and apart from our interest on the IDB side, he wanted to extract his meed of taxes. He was a man of action. Early in March he sent out a circular letter to suspects, requiring a full disclosure of remittances from overseas within one month. Panic spread throughout the Freetown diamond racket, and several leading suspects made preparations to emigrate to Liberia. One Lebanese trader let it be known that he was prepared to find £50,000, but whether as a bribe or as tax he didn't explain. Unfortunately, a group of Ministers complained to the Governor that the demand note was upsetting the country's trade and might lead to trouble, and the Commissioner was called to heel and made to withdraw his circular.

'IDSO, Freetown's comment was that the Government might just as well have issued orders to the Customs not to search IDBs at the airport on the grounds that they might be caught and jailed and have their diamonds seized and thus affect local trade.

'As 1955 sped on, things went from worse to worse in the territory, though various means of tightening up security at the mines began to take effect and production had increased from 25,000 carats in December 1954, to 42,000 carats in July 1955. Morgan caught quite a lot of thieves in the mines, but there was an endless supply of them. After an arrest, production would immediately improve but then die away again as another thief took over. The chaos in the country was affecting Morgan's African guards, particularly in the Concentrator House, where the stones passed through the final stages of recovery and sorting. For instance, one day Morgan arrested the senior guard, together with a grease-table boy, and found 24 carats of diamonds in their pockets. Both men cheerfully pleaded guilty and paid a fine of £300 without turning a hair.

'But these losses were nothing compared with the wholesale rape of the diamond soil outside the mines, and finally Selection Trust decided to launch a local buying operation. Lyall, one of their senior prospectors, pitched camp near an illicit site where there were about 300 illegal miners, and on the grounds that he was prospecting, offered these men five shillings a day to dig for him. They were quite happy to do for five shillings a day what they would otherwise be doing for nothing, and when they found that Lyall's prices were better than anything they could get from the Mandingo traders, they were delighted, and dug away with a will. Only the Mandingo and Lebanese buyers in the neighbouring villages were furious. Lyall was flooded with stones, both from the diggings he was "prospecting" and from all over the country, and at the end of the experiment the pattern was set for what was to prove the solution to the whole problem – the setting up by the Diamond Corporation of buying posts throughout Sierra Leone.

'But meanwhile Sierra Leone Selection Trust had been persuaded to surrender their monopoly mining rights. Meetings were going on in London which resulted in September in Selection Trust accepting £1,570,000 for their rights and limiting their lease area to 450 square miles for a maximum period of thirty years. On their side, the

Government proposed to legalize the illegal diggers by giving them mining and prospecting licences, while the Diamond Corporation would set up machinery for the legal purchase of the previously illegal stones.

'On the whole, although this was certainly unfair to Selection Trust and to the shareholders of the Consolidated African Selection Trust – the Sierra Leone parent company – the scheme was a good one from IDSO's point of view. There would now be no point in smuggling diamonds into Liberia if the native digger could obtain the world price quite legally in Sierra Leone. Short of exterminating the illegal diggers, the only solution was to legalize them. This was duly done, and early last year – on February 6th to be exact – all prosecutions against diamond diggers and dealers were suspended and licensed digging and dealing began. By the end of March fifteen hundred mining licences had been issued and the number later rose to around five thousand, and licences were issued to dealers, one of whom, I was interested to note, was our old friend Finkle, who had lost no time in returning to Freetown from Beirut and setting up shop.

'The sole export licence was granted to the Diamond Corporation, and I was astonished at the way they coped with the problem of swallowing up this huge new flood of stones. They opened trading posts at Freetown and in the interior at Bo and Kenema, built houses for the staff and fixed up air and radio communications. They manned these posts with junior valuers – young University Englishmen under the overall command of an experienced diamond man, and flung them out into the bush with thousands of pounds

in bank-notes. The responsibility and danger were consider-
able. The native miners and dealers insisted on being paid in
cash, and there was no question of getting a second opinion
on a value. One young man, just arrived from England, was
awoken one night by a Negro with a huge diamond wrapped
in a dirty handkerchief. Without hesitation – but I guess with
trepidation – the young man offered him £10,000, and the
notes were forthwith counted out on the table and the Negro
disappeared again into the night. The possibility of making
an expensive mistake with a stone of that size was great,
but I'm glad to say the young man's valuation was accurate,
and he earned great kudos with the Corporation.

'As an example of the flood, during the first three months
of its dealing the Diamond Corporation bought £600,000
worth of diamonds at Bo alone, and since then the total of
these jungle purchases has swollen into millions.

'Today, although IDB into Liberia still goes on, it's not
as bad as it was in the days when we came on the scene, and
the exports from Sierra Leone have leapt astronomically.
For instance, in 1955, before the new regime, the diamond
exports from Sierra Leone amounted to £1,400,000. Last year
the figure was about three million, and when more trading
posts are opened and the outlying territories are brought
into the legal channels, the total annual figure is likely to be
double that. These figures can't be very palatable to Selection
Trust shareholders who have been forced to sell their
seventy-seven-year rights for a mere one and a half million,
but at least the buyers in Liberia, Beirut and Antwerp have
been put out of business and the war against the biggest

smuggling leak in the world is on the way to being won.'

Blaize smiled grimly. 'Or, rather, not quite. Here's a cutting from the officially sponsored *West Africa* of May 5th, 1956:'

> The news that diamonds reported to be worth £750,000 have been seized by the French West African Police in Dakar from two air travellers, an Austrian and a Lebanese, en route from Monrovia, makes us wonder just how successful our new arrangements for mining and marketing diamonds are. For there is little doubt that these diamonds came from Sierra Leone even if that will be difficult to prove . . . .
>
> Since the Diamond Corporation began buying diamonds in February there have been rumours that their purchases were much lower than expected. But the truth seems to be that the Corporation are buying a very high proportion of diamonds being won by Sierra Leoneans who have licences to mine; on the other hand there is still a great deal of illicit mining, since it takes time for the new scheme of licensed local diggers to be put into effect all over the country . . . In the long run the Corporation MUST win. It really VALUES stones and pays for them according to their value.

'As you can see, there were still some big leaks to be closed, and tomorrow I'll tell you about the last shots IDSO fired before we packed our knapsacks and left the battlefield.'

'MONSIEUR DIAMANT'

IT WAS OUR LAST DAY TOGETHER. THE SUN WAS SHINING and we decided to hire a car and drive out for luncheon to the Grottoes of Hercules, just south of Cape Spartel, where the Mediterranean sweeps out through the Straits of Gibraltar into the Atlantic.

On the way we made a detour through the so-called Diplomatic Forest – about ten square miles of eucalyptus and cork trees and mimosas in bloom. Apart from solitary men or women in the fields we met no living thing except an occasional tortoise crossing the road and from time to time a pair of mating storks, which made a brief run and took off gracefully at the noise of the car.

It is a curious corner of the world. Here, among Roman and Phoenician ruins and scattered encampments of Moors and Berbers and Riffs, is one of the great centres of the world's radio communications. The skyline is everywhere pierced by the radio masts of RCA and Mackay and by the pylons in the closely guarded compound from which the Voice of America speaks to Europe and penetrates the Iron Curtain. For some reason this romantic top left-hand corner of the African continent is ideal for radio reception and transmission, and as we drove peacefully along we could imagine the air above us alive with whispering voices – an uncanny feeling.

The Grottoes of Hercules and the near-by reconstructed Roman village where, our driver assured us, Hercules had lived, was not much as tourist attractions go, and we sent the car away and spent the morning trudging along the empty, endless sands that disappeared in the heat haze in the direction of Casablanca, 200 miles to the south.

The levanter had blown shoals of Portuguese men-of-war on to the beach. It amused Blaize to stamp on their poisonous-looking violet bladders as we went along, and his talk was punctuated with what sounded like small-calibre revolver shots.

His story was nearly finished, and as we walked along he emptied his pockets of the notes and scraps of paper he had used to jog his memory and document his story over the previous days. These he tore up into small pieces, occasionally stopping to throw them into the surf and watch them being pulped by the waves.

Any writer would have appreciated the scene – the two lonely figures striding along the immense empty sweep of beach with the African continent on our left hand and, on our right, across the water, the Americas. And the agent destroying his records.

As we walked south into the sun, like two people in the dream sequence of a film, Blaize wound up his story:

'While all this was going on on the African continent, IDSO hadn't been idle in Europe and the Middle East. I'd been concerned entirely with the producing end – stopping the smuggling and IDB at its source, and I think you'll agree that we'd been pretty successful. In the process we'd built up huge intelligence files and a card index of over 5000 names, and IDSO was in constant contact with London and Paris and Antwerp, trying to block up the receiving end in Europe.

'Of course we could do nothing about parcels of stones which had been legally exported, like the flood from Liberia, but there were subsidiary streams flowing northwards that I could often warn, say IDSO Paris, about, and hope that something could be done about them from their end. Sometimes Paris and Antwerp would get advance information of parcels being dispatched and the process was reversed.

'Very soon a picture of the big operators in Europe began to emerge, and particularly of the biggest of all, whom I'll call "Monsieur Diamant". Of course this isn't his real name, but it's the name, or rather title, we gave him.'

Blaize stopped in his tracks. He looked at me and smiled wryly. 'You've written about some pretty good villains in your books, but truth is stranger, etc., and none of your villains stands up to Monsieur Diamant. I should say he's the biggest crook in Europe, if not in the world – not only big, but completely successful. He's getting on now, must be over sixty, a big, hard chunk of a man with about ten million pounds in the bank.

'We think he's a German by origin. He's one of the most respected citizens of Europe – and certainly the most feared – and if I were to tell you all I know about him, and you were to publish it, and you happened to find yourself in his neighbourhood, he'd have you bumped off.'

I said: 'I don't believe it.'

Blaize shrugged his shoulders. 'Well, I'm not going to take a chance. I'm not even going to tell you his real name or where he lives, so that you won't be tempted to start sniffing around. I'm not exaggerating about this man, and you must simply take it as read and we'll get on with the story.'

Blaize started walking on again down the beach. 'Well, the great thing about Monsieur Diamant is that he's completely respectable. He's a name to conjure with in many communities beside the diamond world. Just after the war, when the diamond business was reorganizing itself and it was important for him to get his own machine working again, he was always flying over to London. He'd suddenly appear in the best suite in the grandest hotel. It wasn't easy to live well in London in those days, so Monsieur Diamant used to bring over his own raw meat and butter and cream and so on, and get it cooked for him by the hotel chef. In the evenings, he'd keep open house for his cronies with endless champagne and caviar and half a dozen girls that some agent used to procure for him. They always had to be young, and they were paid fifty pounds a night each. I don't know if they thought it was worth it. Monsieur Diamant had peculiar ways with girls – not a very attractive man, really.

'That's all by the way, so that you can get a picture of the chap, but the point is that most big packets of illegal diamonds getting into Europe end up with him. He's the big fence, and has been for twenty years, and first the Germans and now the Russians and Chinese know it, and deal with him direct.

'He uses Antwerp as one of his headquarters and from there he has three routes through the Iron Curtain, and he has a team of professional couriers who carry for him. These people get fat salaries, but he also insures them and their families against loss of revenue during prison sentence, gets them new passports if their own are confiscated, and generally looks after their welfare.

'His routes are, first by Russian and Polish ships from the port of Antwerp, secondly to cover addresses in Switzerland, and thirdly to West Berlin for passage through to the East.

'He's not the only one, of course, but he's by far the biggest and the best organized, and he was our main target in Europe.'

I said: 'How big is this traffic through the Iron Curtain? And why does it exist, anyway? Only the other day the Russians put out that they had discovered huge new diamond fields somewhere inside the Arctic Circle – on a tributary of the Vilyui.'

'No one's ever seen anything to back that story up, and at any rate the Diamond Corporation don't think there's anything new in it. If the Russians have got all that supply on tap, why would they be paying above world prices in Liberia

and Belgium, as we know they're doing? It happens that
we've got a contact in the Russian zone of Berlin – in the
Trade Ministry there – and just the other day he reported
that for only fourteen days in February this year nearly half a
million pounds' worth of illegal diamonds had been smuggled over from West Berlin and from Hanau and Brucken
and Idar Oberstein, which is where the Germans have their
diamond-cutting industry.

'Most of the stones were from Africa and the rest from
Brazil, and most of them were industrial diamonds. They had
been smuggled or bought all over the world. They usually
originated in Antwerp, but some came from Holland and
America and even England, and there was a trickle from
Israel and Italy.

'Our man in East Berlin said that the destination of about
a quarter of these stones was Russia. Another quarter went
to China, and the rest was divided up among the other
Communist countries – all presumably for the various
armament industries.

'That's a whole lot of diamonds in a fortnight, and if it's
typical, it adds up to about twelve million pounds' worth a
year. That's not an impossible figure, but it does suggest that
the Russians are pretty keen on the trade.

'Anyway, our main object in Europe was to do everything we could to upset Monsieur Diamant's sources of
supply and also the leaks through the rest of Europe, and a
lot of our work in Africa consisted of tipping off London
or Antwerp or Paris whenever we got wind of a fat parcel
on its way out of Africa towards Monsieur Diamant or his

friends. There was nothing we could do against him personally. That's what I mean about him being the greatest crook
in Europe. In all his thirty years or so of operating, he's
never slipped up with a conviction. At European police
headquarters, the only thing you'd find on his file would
be that he made fat subscriptions to the police welfare and
athletic clubs. It's only the various Secret Services that know
about him. But that doesn't worry him. He's above the law —
a really formidable operator.

'Mark you,' said Blaize, and at once he became the
careful, fair-minded lawyer, talking legal jargon, 'occasionally it happened that an entirely innocent trader came under
suspicion when we were trying to plug these leaks out of
Africa. Perhaps this was inevitable because acts which are
in fact infringements of the Customs laws are by no means
always distinguishable by moral turpitude on the part of the
offender. This is not to condone breaches of the Customs
law when they are proved, but simply to say that the laws
of most countries, especially the Customs laws, are so highly
complex, that sometimes the determination of the legality
or otherwise of certain acts in the course of international
trading is not a thing that can be decided in a moment. That
goes for other offences too. So it's no reflection on the
persons taking part in legal proceedings or the investigations
leading up to them that it's sometimes only after a good
deal of argumentation that an unfortunate trader suspected
either of a crime or an infringement of the civil law, but
guiltless of both, gets his innocence proclaimed.

'One such case was that of Philip Schreiber. Schreiber

was, as it turned out, in perfectly lawful possession of certain diamonds. By now, however, IDSO had its finger so firmly on the pulse of the world diamond trade that often it could not only follow but also forecast the movement of both illegitimate and legitimate diamonds. So it was that IDSO, as a matter of routine, were able to tell the customs at Yoff Airport, Dakar, of the impending arrival of diamonds to the value of 18,000 carats on the person of one P. Schreiber. Schreiber arrived at Dakar with his diamonds, as forecast early in April 1956. A dispute arose about their liability to duty, and the outcome was that Schreiber was detained for six weeks at Dakar, and was then released on what the French call "provisional liberty" which is a form of bail without a money bond – in other words, freedom pending the hearing of the case. Meanwhile the diamonds in question had been valued by experts, who eventually estimated their value at £120,000, though their original estimate had been as much as £900,000.

'When the case came on, at first the decision went against Schreiber, but he appealed. A year later, the Appeal Court found that the diamonds were being conveyed in transit, and it was only because the plane had been delayed in Dakar that they had not continually been so.' [N.B. In fact, on May 15th, Schreiber was acquitted *purement et simplement*. The Court had ordered that the diamonds be restored to him. And so they were. Schreiber came out of it all without a stain on his character. I.F.]

'In 1956 three other cases began, all of which resulted in the traders involved establishing their innocence. On

September 6th, 1955, on, as they say, 'information received', IDSO, London, had telephoned IDSO, Paris, to say that two men called Amschel Benny Engel and Solomon Cukrowicz would shortly be leaving Monrovia for Paris. They would be carrying with them a large quantity of diamonds. They were to take the Air France service from Dakar to Orly Airport – the famous "Etoile de Dakar" flight – and would arrive there on September 17th.

'As a matter of routine we passed this information to M. Lallet, Commissaire de la Police de l'Air. Cukrowicz and Engel duly arrived with their diamonds, and also a third passenger by the name of David Gollansky, who had declared a package he had with him as containing rough diamonds. The package bore the seal of the Government of Liberia. Our man went over to Orly with M. Mario Pinci, the French diamond expert. M. Pinci examined Cukrowicz's and Engel's diamonds, and pronounced them to be of Sierra Leonean origin, amounting to 265 carats and valued at £9500. Our man, supported by the police, as an officer of IDSO and as a representative of Selection Trust, made a formal claim to the stones on the ground that they were the property of his buying company and must at one time or another have been stolen.

'Gollansky's packet was not opened, but, to cut a long story short, a charge was subsequently made by Selection Trust against Cukrowicz and Engel and Gollansky of theft and receiving *vol et recel*.

'Cukrowicz, Engel and Gollansky first saw examining magistrates on September 16th. In the end a *non-lieu* was returned on June 12th, 1956, and it was confirmed by the

Chambre de Mise en Accusation – that's roughly the French equivalent of a Grand Jury – on October 19th, 1956. In other words, the case was dismissed and the diamonds returned to the men. All three, Cukrowicz, Engel and Gollansky, had been in lawful possession, and their honesty was established.

'Then,' continued Blaize, doffing, much to my relief, his wig and gown, 'in 1956 two successful coups came off in quick succession at different points in West Africa, each of which was in small or large degree made possible by IDSO.

'In the first case, one of the big couriers tripped up. This was an Indian whose principal was financed by Hungary. Incidentally he possessed a British passport issued in Monrovia, as well as two Indian passports issued in Cairo and Damascus. He was a regular traveller between Liberia and Beirut whom we'd been watching. On this occasion he had been for some months in Monrovia, and steadily buying industrial diamonds at prices well above the market. Now he was on his way out, and he had got as far as Conakry Airport in French West Africa, in transit to Paris and Budapest.

'The Director of Customs at Conakry was tipped off. When he was interrogated, the Indian cheerfully yielded up his parcel and triumphantly pointed out that it bore the seal of the Bureau of Mines of Monrovia and the signature of the Director of the Bureau. When asked what the packet contained he foolishly said that there were a mere 800 stones, instead of the true and majestic total of 119,000, which were subsequently valued at £35,000.

'The courier wasn't charged with any offence, but his diamonds were seized and he was ignominiously packed off back to Monrovia. Shortly thereafter, his principal, the dealer acting for Hungary, flew down to visit him, and I can imagine that the occasion must have been extremely unpleasant for him.

'The heat was kept on, and in the same eventful month another bird fell. This was a certain Alhaji Mustafa Ibrahim, the bearer of three British passports issued in Lagos, Accra and Dakar, and travel certificates issued in Lagos and Freetown. In the days when our old friend Finkle of Freetown was a prohibited immigrant, this character acted as his courier with Beirut, and we'd often wanted to catch up with him. Now, on April 24th, he arrived at Accra Airport from Freetown with a policeman as his shadow. At the airport, Mustafa hired a taxi driver named Alio Giwa to take him over the frontier into French West Africa, and the Gold Coast police, under the instructions of their well-known Commissioner, Mike Collins, chased after him and stopped his car just before the frontier village of Aflao. The car was searched and a parcel of diamonds weighing 712 carats was found taped to the steering column. Mustafa came up for trial and his diamonds were confiscated. He was also sent to jail for eight months on a charge of obtaining one of his many passports under false pretences – a sentence which caused many of his friends to weep in court.

'And so, in a brief blaze of glory and to much weeping and gnashing of teeth in Monrovia and among Monsieur Diamant's friends in Europe, IDSO wound up its activities and prepared to disband.

'Once the Diamond Corporation had set itself up in

Sierra Leone and was ousting the IDB by straight commercial methods there was nothing more for us to do that couldn't be done by the mine security staffs and by the local police forces in Africa. The next few months were spent tidying up loose ends and discussing with De Beers the retention of a skeleton organization to keep a watching brief. After the excitement of the previous two years and the tension there was nothing but anticlimax as our men gradually drifted off to other jobs. Some have gone back to intelligence or security work and others to appointments with De Beers and the Anglo-American Corporation.

'So far as I'm concerned' – Blaize shrugged his shoulders – 'I'm sick of crooks and sick of spying on them. All I want is a nice quiet job as a country lawyer or administrator in a university, or some other job where I can clear all this muck out of my mind.'

He grinned. 'As you said in the last sentence of one of your books: "It reads better than it lives."'

POSTSCRIPT

EARLY NEXT MORNING I WENT TO THE AIRPORT TO SEE Blaize off. It was drizzling out of a sullen sky and the drab Moroccan landscape was more squalid than usual. Inside the dirty white cement building there was the usual early morning smell of cheap airports – a mixture of coffee, petrol, sweat and old tobacco smoke. The frontier police and the Customs officials looked as if they had slept in their clothes and there was sleep-dirt in the corners of their hard suspicious eyes.

Blaize was flying to Nice and taking the train on to Monte Carlo. There, with the help of a book on roulette systems and a hundred pounds, he proposed to wash the last three years and the African continent out of his system in forty-eight hours of old-fashioned Riviera high life. Then he would take the train for London, play golf for a month to complete the cure, and decide what to do next.

I was sorry he was going. From the first I had liked him and, in a week of listening to his story, I had grown to admire him. I admire professionals, and Blaize was a professional to his fingertips. More important, he had those qualities which one likes to find in one's compatriots – courage, humour, imagination, common sense and a warm heart. It had been odd to find these qualities in a spy.

We said goodbye and arranged to meet again. Blaize, a macintosh over his very English clothes, but without a hat, joined the few other passengers who had found it necessary to travel on Easter Sunday, and filed out past the Air France stewardess with the check list.

I heard him say his name. He turned and gave me a farewell grin and walked out into the rain.

I went to the open door and watched the four engines of the Constellation kick and fire one by one. The rain hadn't yet laid the sand on the runway and as the big plane moved away for the takeoff a stinging hurricane raised by the propellers caught me in the face. I dodged behind the glass and mopped at my face with a handkerchief. I was still wiping grit from my eyes as I heard the roar of the plane taking off.

I smiled to myself as I walked out of the airport to my taxi. It seemed typical of this bizarre week that at the end of the play the secret agent should have vanished off-stage in a cloud of dust.

Towards the end of June, I got a letter from Blaize. There was nothing in the envelope but a cutting from the *Daily Telegraph* of June 19th. This is what it said:

SMUGGLER'S £39,000 GEMS SEIZED BY CUSTOMS
HATTON GARDEN MAN FINED £5000 AND SENT TO
PRISON

From Our Special Correspondent
Belfast, Tuesday

Diamonds valued at £39,784 were produced in the
Custody Court, Belfast, today. NATHAN ASCHER GLATT,
36, former Dutch Jewish refugee who was given asylum
in England, of Claremont Park, Finchley, pleaded guilty
to attempting to export them illegally to the Republic
of Ireland.

He was sentenced to nine months' imprisonment,
fined £5000 and ordered to serve an additional three
months' imprisonment in default of payment. He also
forfeits the diamonds.

The court was told by Mr. R. F. Sheldon, the Crown
Solicitor, that the diamonds were discovered 'on Glatt's
body'. His interrogation lasted about fourteen hours.

In all 716 diamonds were concealed in two rubber-
covered packages. Photographs handed to the magistrates showed the packages to be about two inches long
and one and a quarter inches in diameter.

Mr. Sheldon said that Glatt produced the diamonds
only after a search warrant had been obtained from a
Justice of the Peace. An examination was conducted
by Dr. H. P. Lowe, City Coroner, and Mr. H. Rogers,
Professor of Surgery at Queen's University, Belfast.

For the prosecution Mr. Sheldon explained that the

Irish Republic was one of the countries to which the export of diamonds was prohibited. Last Monday week, he said, Mr. H. J. Browning, deputy chief investigating officer, Customs and Excise, London, saw Glatt arrive at London Airport early in the morning.

He booked a single ticket to Belfast in the name of Harris and was followed on to the aircraft. At Belfast Airport he was seen to go into the lavatories.

Afterwards he went to the railway station and booked a first-class ticket to Dublin, but was taken off the train by Customs officers. He denied that he had any diamonds concealed. He refused to allow a doctor to examine him. 'I am not having my body violated,' he said. Later, after permission had been granted by a Justice of the Peace, Glatt was taken to a nursing home. 'After he again refused, he was held and examined,' said Mr. Sheldon. He then produced the diamonds. The diamonds he was carrying had been traced from their origin in South Africa to their arrival in Glatt's possession. Customs investigators had watched the courier who was to pick them up from Glatt at a Dublin hotel pass through London Airport on his way to the rendezvous. From that moment Glatt's every move was recorded.

Across the top of the cutting Blaize had pencilled: *Who wouldn't rather play golf?*

penguin.co.uk/vintage